WORK YOUR WEALTH

9 STEPS
TO MAKING SMARTER CHOICES
WITH YOUR MONEY

BY MARY BETH STORJOHANN, CF

Disclaimer: The advice and strategies contained herein may not be suitable for every situation. This work is sold with the understanding that the Author and Publisher are not engaged in rendering legal or accounting services. Neither the Author nor the Publisher shall be liable for damages arising here from. The fact that an organization or website is referred to in this work as a citation or a potential source of further information does not mean that the Author or the Publisher endorses the information that the organization or website may provide or recommendations it may make. Further, readers should be aware that Internet websites listed in this work may have changed or disappeared between when this work was written and when it is read. Names and identifying details have been changed to protect the privacy of individuals.

Paperback ISBN: 978-0-692-62733-4

Cover and Book Design: Melody Christian, Finicky Designs

Editing by: Kali Hawlk

For Brian:

Thank you for being my number one fan and for giving me the courage to push boundaries and pursue dreams I never thought imaginable.

For Andrea:

Thank you for being my person.

Contents

Foreword

Over the last seven years I've studied what it means to live an "intentional life" through books, religious philosophies, courses, and guests from all walks of life on my podcast, The Lively Show. Along the way, I've discovered most people use the word *intention* in one of three ways:

The first use of the word "intention" is as a substitute for the word "goal," as in, "It's my intention to deposit $10,000 into my 401(k) this year." An intention is set and then worked towards.

The second use of the word is associated with the general idea of being deliberate. For example, "I'm intentionally creating a budget." All focus is going towards completing a certain activity with care, attention and detail.

And lastly, my favorite (and perhaps most transformational) use of the term is to describe a person's deepest values in a particular area of their lives. I've named this final use of the word a "values-based intention" to differentiate it from the first and second definitions.

An example of a financial values-based intention may be, "to have a stable and secure financial life," or "to optimize the resources I have at hand given my current circumstances." Values-based intentions are prevalent in all areas of our lives, finances included.

When focusing on our core values, a myriad of ways to embody those values may be possible and available – to the point that it can feel downright overwhelming to pick a direction to move forward with! So even with a clear(ish) vision and set goals of what we desire, we can still have a hard time connecting that vision to plan of action.

This is especially common when it comes to our financial life. We find ourselves aware of what's important to us in certain areas of our lives, like being able to take a chance on a career change, or launching a business, or perhaps being more available to spend time traveling or with family, but we're unsure of how to handle those leaps and transitions and the risk that may come with it based on our current financial situation and resources.

So what do many of us often do? We simply move forward hoping "it will all work out in the end" – but never really knowing if we are doing what is truly in our best financial interest. And while we might look like we have it all together on the outside, an internal whisper of self-doubt may permeate our thoughts and purchases.

That's where Mary Beth comes in.

As a Millennial and CERTIFIED FINANCIAL PLANNER™, Mary Beth is able to bridge the gap between what is most important to us as Millennials, and the steps that we need to take to support ourselves financially given the quickly evolving retirement landscape, the rise of self-generated income, and more.

With Mary Beth's guidance, we will be able to not only feel peaceful and confident about our financial choices, but we will know that they are aligned with what is most important to us on levels far deeper than money itself.

Because the truth is we want to thrive in all areas of our lives. And our financial well-being intersects and enables many aspects of our careers, travels, families, and homes. We deserve to educate ourselves on our financial options so that we can move forward in alignment with our values, using the practices that best support them.

Mary Beth will show us the way.

With love,
Jess!

An Invitation

Working your wealth isn't something that happens overnight.

It takes time, perseverance, dedication and in some cases what feels like an army to get things on track. This book was written to provide you with a step-by-step guide in how to take control of your money. Each chapter has a list of Money Moves and recommended activities, and the actions build upon each other, until *voila!* Your money is organized and on track.

In order to help you tackle these exercises and give your finances the swift kick in the butt it may need, I stashed some great resources over at www.workyourwealthbook.com. You can head there to gain access to guides, templates, and some checklists that will help you ditch the stress around money once and for all.

In addition to the resources available at www.workyourwealthbook.com, if you're looking for a safe place to learn, share and grow around your finances, I've created a Work Your Wealth community *just* for you! Once you've signed up for the book resources at the site above, just click the link in your e-mail to request to join the group. We're setting goals, sharing tips, getting advice, and celebrating wins on a daily basis. I'd love if you wanted to join our conversation!

Are you ready to Work Your Wealth? Here we go!

Introduction

For a majority of my life, I hated to talk about money. It made me uncomfortable. Even from an early age, money stressed me out. I was consistently concerned with how items would be paid for, whether or not I had enough room in my budget, and the idea of running out of cash completely.

I wasn't raised in a household where my parents sat me down and taught me about the time value of money, how to invest early, or why it was so important to save. I grew up in a household where money *was* talked about, but the conversations were often loud and sometimes heated. There never seemed to be enough money, and it was a paycheck-to-paycheck situation for as long as I could remember. My parents loved each other and my sisters and me, but we were in a constant cycle of financial catch-up. Even though I may not have understood the concepts and numbers completely, I picked up on the stress my family felt around money at an early age and carried it with me into my late 20s – well into my career in personal finance.

According to the American Psychological Association, an August 2014 survey of 3,068 adults found that 72 percent felt stressed about money at least part of the time with 54 percent saying they had "just enough" or not enough money at the end of the month to make ends meet.[1] Finances are a tough topic for many, and I wasn't alone in my experience.

---

[1] http://jobs.aol.com/articles/2015/02/04/stress-levels-down-apa-survey/

As I grew older, I discovered friends who grew up in similar situations. I started a blog early in my career and found others who were trying to build a different path for themselves. I launched Workable Wealth in 2013 and began to speak with members of Gen Y and Gen X across the United States – and even abroad – who grew up with a lack of financial education and clarity and were now being faced with the prospect of heading down a similar path or trying to figure it out on their own. Many of them were asking the same question: ***How?***

- How do you get a handle on your money when the mere prospect of talking about it gives you anxiety?

- How do you get yourself on track when you don't know the right questions to ask?

- How do you navigate the crazy finance lingo, the accounts that are behind on payments or that should be opened and aren't, and the ridiculous amount of time it takes to get organized?

- How do you manage every aspect of your financial life?

It wasn't until my sophomore year of college that I learned you *can* control money instead of letting it control you. I had landed a job as a receptionist in a local wealth management firm, and my workspace placed me front and center to some of the best client interaction. I saw many tired, anxious faces initially arrive for their meetings and noticed how those same faces would be relaxed and relieved when they left. I began to understand the work that was being done and that there was an entire career and industry that revolved around helping people get financially fit. That was 2004. I was in!

My parents may not have been able to teach me about interest rates and investments, but what they did teach me was the power of a hard day's work. I got my first job at the age of 15 and never looked back. From telemarketing and making pizzas at Papa John's to working the counter at a local Italian eatery, a dry cleaner, and more, I hustled my way through high school (sometimes working two jobs at once). I paid for yearbooks, clothes, gas, prom tickets, and most other items one would want as a teenager with my own money.

Both of my parents worked while my sisters and I grew up. My dad sometimes held two or three jobs at one time. He'd come home exhausted at the end of the day, but it was humbling to see the lengths he and my mom went to in order to provide for us. I learned early on that there aren't many handouts that will come your way. If you want something, you have to have the drive and determination to work for it – and that includes handling your finances.

WHY I WROTE THIS BOOK

When I launched Workable Wealth, my desire was to help people in their 20s, 30s and 40s across the country make smarter choices with their money. I was tired of my generation being ignored by the personal finance industry. I was put off by the outdated information touted by people my grandparents' age – and frankly, I was 100% irritated with the media's stance that our generation "didn't want financial advice."

I was lucky enough to actually major in *money* in college. Not surprisingly, however, most people have other passions to pursue. I realized early on that there's a huge disconnect between today's education system and financial planning firms and the availability and accessibility of financial information and guidance for this age group. Translation: There is none.

After 12 years in the personal finance industry, one of the biggest things I've learned is that people need clear-cut guidance. It's exhausting to sit through meetings full of fancy lingo or to spend hours digging through online articles trying to figure out where to start and which advice is the best advice or applies to your unique situation. The internet can only offer up so much information. Of the hundreds upon hundreds of conversations I've had with my peers and those looking to get on track financially, it all comes down to wanting and needing a set action plan of steps to take and a clue on where to begin.

This book is meant to provide just that. It will cut through the crap, lay out an organized plan of attack, break down steps into specific homework assignments along the way, and leave you with clarity and confidence in your financial life. Each chapter will close with a list of Money Moves you need to make to get started in each area and will direct you on how to proceed. We'll focus on real, actionable, and specific steps you can take now.

This book will dig into the "how" behind each step and leave you with easy-to-follow directions in applying each action to your life. At the end of each chapter, you'll have completed a piece of your very own personal financial plan, leaving you that much closer to reaching your goals.

THIS BOOK IS FOR YOU IF YOU'RE:

- Ready to figure out where your money is going and redirect it to the areas that matter most to you

- Willing to learn, do the work, and get a little uncomfortable

- Looking for clarity, confidence, and a plan around your money, but aren't sure how to proceed

- In your 20s to 40s and are tired of feeling intimidated by fancy industry lingo, old men behind mahogany desks, and people making you feel like you need to have more money to deserve a plan to take care of it

- Experiencing any kind of life transition such as getting married, having children, changing jobs, moving cities, buying a new home, and more

- Looking to tackle your debt with a strategy to eliminate it

- Ready to start saving for your future – even with the smallest amount

- Wanting to invest and build your nest egg for retirement

THIS BOOK ISN'T FOR YOU IF YOU'RE:

- Transitioning to retirement

- Looking for complicated Social Security distribution strategies

- In need of an in-depth analysis of historical stock market returns

- Not into having fun

- Looking for a quick fix for your finances and aren't ready to be held accountable in getting your money organized

- Convinced you'll "just figure it out" along the way

WHAT YOU'LL FIND IN THE PAGES

One of the things I tell my clients is that along with crafting a financial plan and laying out the steps to get you launched on your personal money journey, I'm also going to be your coach and accountability partner. I'll make it fun and friendly, but I'm also going to be direct. If you're in financial trouble because of some bad decisions, lack of education, or whatever the reason, we'll address the issue to ensure the course can be corrected going forward. From there, we're going to move the heck on. There's no room for dwelling in the past when it comes to money moves gone wrong.

Taking control of your finances can be fun and I strive to make it so, but you also need to be prepared to show up and put forth the effort. Trust me: This. Will. Be. Work. I'm not saying to shut down your schedule for the next six months, but if you're not willing to devote a few hours or an afternoon to digging into your money situation, you're likely not ready to take control of it.

I'm a big proponent of breaking down big steps into little steps, measuring progress and celebrating wins along the way. This book is laid out in such a way that each chapter addresses a bigger overall topic in your financial health. Within each section is a list of steps to get you set up within each area. While you can hop around between topics if you'd like, my recommendation is to work through the book in chronological order as each chapter helps to deepen and build a foundation around your money story and will serve as information in helping you become organized in subsequent chapters.

THE MESSAGES IN 9 STEPS TO WORKABLE WEALTH

What you want matters. With FOMO (fear of missing out), a very real issue in today's society, it's time to figure out what you really want in your life. No comparison games, no outside pressure. When you dig in and figure out the kind of life you're passionate about living, it makes aligning your money with those goals so much easier.

Where your money goes matters. I'm not all about cutting lattes and living without cable (unless that's what you want, which is totally okay). Your spending plan is about *conscious* decision making. If you decide that you want a lifestyle that includes daily lattes, more power to you! So what are you willing to give up in *other* areas to make that happen? Want to travel abroad every year? Awesome! Are you up for living in a smaller apartment or trading in your SUV to get there? Understanding where your money is going will help you to make the conscious decisions needed to ensure you can redirect it to the areas that matter most to number one: *you.*

Report cards never really go away. Your credit score is your financial report card that will follow you for the rest of your life, saving – or costing – you money along the way. We're talking thousands of dollars. It's a grade that really matters, making it important that you have a debt knockout strategy in place, knowledge of what your grade is, and how you can improve or maintain your score.

Mistakes happen. Learn from them and move on. Don't dwell. You can't change the past.

You matter. Whether single or paired off, kids or no kids, you matter. The love you provide and receive from friends and family makes it essential to have an estate plan and documents in place should something happen to you. The income and financial support you receive or provide makes it imperative that you protect those assets. Insurance may not be a glamorous topic, but if you get injured on the job and can't work, you're going to wish you had disability income protection. You matter, and it's important to look out for yourself and your loved ones by making sure you check the right boxes to ensure everyone is protected.

It's never too late or too early to start. Whether it's doing an initial review, making monthly money dates with yourself, setting up your Roth IRA contributions, finally taking advantage of your employer's 401(k) match, or beginning to save that first $1,000 in your emergency fund, just get started. Don't worry about the path to getting there or the length of time it will take. Automate your savings and get started as soon as possible. The earlier you start saving towards your goals and your future, the better off you'll be.

HOW THIS BOOK IS LAID OUT

Step 1: You'll figure out the kind of life you want to live. You'll answer questions about your values and set a minimum of three short- and long-term goals for yourself.

Step 2: You'll put your money where your heart is. Now that your goals are set and you've determined what's important to you, you'll begin to analyze where your money is going and bust your bad money habits. You'll create a spending plan for yourself that ditches the deprivation and makes room for your past, present and future.

Step 3: You'll get credit savvy. You'll learn why your score is important, the factors that are likely affecting you, and how to make improvements. You'll pull your credit report and learn what to look for when reviewing it and how to use the score to your advantage.

Step 4: You'll kick your debt to the curb – for good! You'll learn what you need to know about your debt, how to find that information, the best repayment plan for your situation, and how to ensure you stay out of the red going forward.

Step 5: You'll learn how to manage and track your financial health, shape up your account organization to clearly track assets and debts, and the key rules of thumb to keep in mind along the way for spending and saving.

Step 6: You'll learn about your money's best friend, investing for your future, the power of starting today, how to calculate the amount you need to save, and the right kinds of accounts to take advantage of. We'll also touch on some of the frequently asked questions I come across in regards to investing.

Step 7: You'll learn about the power of protection. No one likes thinking about anything bad happening, but the fact is it could, and it might. Figure out the types of insurance you do and don't need, considerations to make for the amounts, and what forms you need to have in place to ensure your wishes are documented.

Step 8: You'll learn how to invest in yourself. Your income is one of your biggest assets (if not the biggest) so it's important that you continue to grow it through investing, negotiating and additional education.

Step 9: You'll learn how to conquer the real-life money issues you're facing daily. Should you rent or own a home? What's the best way to tackle your student loans? How do you handle extra money you might receive? What should you do when a job offer comes your way?

It's important to keep in mind that "wealth" means different things to different people. Whether it's a life of balance between work and family, the ability to travel internationally each year, buying your first home, getting that raise, being debt-free, or reaching "millionaire" status, this book will lay out the steps you need to take and consider in reaching your financial goals and more.

Remember to be kind to yourself along the way. Break down big or overwhelming tasks into smaller to-dos. And don't forget that rarely does anyone's financial picture reflect a straight line to success. The journey to success resembles a jungle gym with ups, downs, and twists and turns along the way – and chances are it's one heck of a ride. Now let's jump in!

Chapter 1:

WHAT KIND OF LIFE DO YOU WANT?

"Money is only a tool. It will take you wherever you wish,
but it will not replace you as the driver." ~ Ayn Rand

Fear of missing out (or FOMO) is a real phenomenon. It refers to the sadness and anxiety you feel when missing out on an event, not being a part of a memory that was made, or having to choose between two activities. As a generation and population that now lives on social media, spending hours refreshing feeds, checking for "likes," and laying filter upon filter onto our photos so that our skin looks flawless and our lives luxurious, it's no wonder that there's so much stress and anxiety around money.

We're bombarded with posts about fabulous jobs, pictures of shiny new cars, glamorous weddings, delicious looking food, happily-ev-er-after families, and more in what can be less than a five-minute period. When it comes to the constant parade of flashy items and success that it appears everyone in our close-knit group of 500 Face-book friends has, it can be hard not to want the same things and to spend our money chasing them.

"Heather is in Europe for three weeks for work? I wish I had a job that paid for me to travel!"

"Sean has a new BMW? I can totally afford one too!"

"Everyone is going on that cruise to Mexico. Why shouldn't I join?"

"Check out Rob and Janelle's wedding photos! We should definitely splurge for the band, three-course meal and open bar. This is our chance to really shine."

Social media and the lives that everyone projects to the world make it extremely difficult to determine what it is you actually want in your *own* life. It's easy to compare and desire the things that somebody else has, when, in fact, those aren't things that will make you happy. We end up throwing our money at objects or experiences that we think we desire before we've even taken the time to figure out what means the most to us. Figuring out what you want to achieve and why you want to achieve it can be a challenge, but it's the best first step you should take to organize your finances.

If you're ready to get clear on your goals and learn how to work towards them, let's map out the kind of life you want.

WHAT'S YOUR WHY?

I can't tell you how many raised eyebrows I received upon launching Workable Wealth. Why give up a steady paycheck and the stability of a growing career? Why not wait a few years? Why focus on a demographic that doesn't "want" the advice? I was hit with a ton of questions. Didn't I know this couldn't be profitable?! There were naysayers galore!

The thing about all the questioning was that it actually turned out to be a blessing. Leading up to the launch of the company, and even now, I've been challenged about the type of business I'm building. This has forced me to hone in on and answer all those "why" questions. It gave me an opportunity to get extremely clear on the reasoning, thoughts and beliefs behind my actions. In the beginning I stumbled over the questions; my answers were shaky and a little unsure. Now my answers are clear, concise, and come with a healthy dose of confidence.

UNDERSTAND WHY YOUR GOALS MATTER TO YOU

Stop for a minute and think about your finances. Is it the tangible items you purchase that motivate you and make you feel successful, or is it the experiences you put your money towards? What are you saving up for right now? Is it new technology, a vacation or a new home? Are you tackling debt and building up your emergency fund? Are you considering switching careers and going back to school?

Whatever it is you're looking to do with your money, ask yourself:

Why is Money Important to You?

There's a term in the financial planning industry called "bag-lady syndrome." This is when a client fears they'll run out of money and end up homeless, living out of a bag. This syndrome causes anxiety, questioning, and a hefty amount of ongoing stress.

How do I know? Not only have I had first-hand experience in working with this cohort of clients (who, by the way, come in all ages and both genders), but I'm also a recovered bag-lady-syndrome sufferer myself. Seeing the kind of stress that money could cause while I was growing up took a hold on my life by giving me the belief that there would never be enough money to do all the things that needed to be done or that I wanted to do. It wasn't until I became clear on why money was important to me and what it represented that I was finally able to overcome my anxiety. It may sound a bit "woo-woo," but money is a tool and you have to figure out the best way it should be utilized in your life.

Today, money represents security for my family. It's a roof over our heads and food on the table. With that security comes peace of mind that we're taken care of. From there, money provides freedom to do more, including helping others, traveling, and embarking on new adventures. Money is a tool that provides comfort, freedom and flexibility. It's a tool that we control and manage for exact purposes. Notice it's not magically providing all of those things. There is a plan in place to direct the money to those areas.

How money is utilized and what it means won't necessarily be the same for you. Money could represent independence from parents or partners in that you're able to support yourself. It could bring confidence in knowing that you're en route to becoming debt-free or security in knowing you're maxing out your retirement accounts.

Take some time to answer the questions below and establish why money is important to you. The things that need to happen in order to make you happy are linked to your "why." And understanding your "why" is what will keep you in line when the roadblocks pop up. It's what will empower you to move forward and is the reason you will meet your goals. It's how you'll show yourself and others that you've got this money thing under control.

- Why are you saving for these items or spending the way you do? Forget the fact that you simply "want it." Why do you feel you need to make these purchases?

- Do you feel secure knowing you have money in the bank? Or do you see that money as a reason to spend as you wish?

- Is there a sense of power and confidence that will come along with being debt-free or taking that next big trip?

- How does reaching your money goals make you feel?

- What's the ultimate reason behind your desire to earn more, save more or experience more? How does it translate into your life?

GOALS, GOALS, GOALS

If you're anywhere near social media these days, you know there's no shortage of inspirational and motivating tweets, pins and posts pushing the importance of goal setting. Maybe you've even seen some of these:

"Setting goals is the first step in turning the invisible into the visible." – Tony Robbins

"A goal properly set is halfway reached." – Zig Ziglar

"Begin with the end in mind." – Stephen Covey

"People with goals succeed because they know where they're going." – Earl Nightingale

Despite all of the hype and push from people like Tony Robbins and Zig Ziglar, the majority of people simply don't set goals for themselves. The even more shocking part (*insert sarcasm here*) is that those who *do* set clear-cut goals become more successful than those who don't. If the life lesson that "goals = success" isn't reason enough for you to jump on the goal-setting bandwagon, consider the fact that measuring results and being intentional about what you want will do more for you than simply throwing it out to the universe that you want something.

When you set goals, you define your dreams for the future. You spell out what motivates you and what you hope to achieve. By defining what you hope to accomplish, you lay out the exact reasons and items that will keep you inspired to staying organized and on track with your finances.

Some of your goals may be things that you want to do in the not-so-distant future, like paying off your credit card debt or buying a new car, while others may be more distant, such as buying a new home. Having specific goals will be the foundation of your financial life. Ultimately, you need to know what you're looking to accomplish before you begin saving or investing. You wouldn't hop in the car and head somewhere without an endpoint in mind, and the same goes for your money. You need to direct it towards something. Setting goals will help you to do just that.

SET THE RIGHT KIND OF GOALS

Chances are you've set a New Year's resolution for yourself once or twice. You probably kicked off January 1st with a super-energized trip to the gym, a "no-spend day," or by sending out twenty resumes because this was the year you'd finally leave behind the job that is sucking the life out of you. Fast forward to April or May and the gym membership went unused, the credit card balances still looked the same, and you couldn't leave your job for a lower-paying one that would make you happier because you didn't know how you'd pay your bills.

Sound familiar?

While your head is in the right space, chances are your approach might be a little bit off. It's easy to throw out some generic goals along the lines of "I'm going to lose weight," "I'm going to start working out more," "I'm going to become debt-free," or "I'm going to start saving for a home." But with goals like that, how do you know if you're on track to achieving them? How do you know when they're actually accomplished?

Which of the goals below seem more achievable and actionable to you?

- ☐ I want to be debt-free.
- ☐ I want to pay off $10,000 of debt in the next three years.

- ☐ I want to buy a house.
- ☐ I want to save $30,000 for a down payment on a house in four years.

- ☐ I want to make more money.
- ☐ I want to grow my income by $5,000 per year over the next two years.

16

I'm hoping you picked the second goal in each set. When it comes to shaping your goals, consider these questions:

- What do I hope to achieve personally, professionally and financially?

- Why are these goals important to me? How will they affect my life?

- Am I ready to make the necessary changes to reach my goals?

- Do these goals reflect my values and no one else's?

- How can I best hold myself accountable?

- What will I do differently this time to ensure success?

One of the questions I ask at every workshop or presentation I give and on every client consultation call I have is: "If we were meeting three years from today, what would have had to happen personally, professionally and financially in order for you to be happy with the progress you've made?"

Guess what usually happens? Dead silence. My favorite times are when I have couples on the call because I make them each answer separately. There's the inevitable dance around "No, you go first," and sometimes I'll even get a "Ditto" from the second spouse. Money can be a *tough* topic for some people to address.

So what do the answers to this three-year question usually look like? Let's look at a real-life example. Check out these responses from a couple we'll call Katie and Roger, who are 29 and 30 and have been married for two years:

Katie said:

- I will have been promoted to a different job.
- We would like to own a house.
- We will have money in our savings account and won't be living paycheck to paycheck.

- We will be debt-free, aside from student loans.
- Personally, we will have started our family.

Roger said:

- I will continue career progression as is.
- Financially, I hope to have put aside money into my company retirement plan.
- We will have a successful, diversified portfolio.
- We will have a minimum of $10,000 in a savings account.
- We will own a home and be ready to start a family.
- We would be debt-free.

While three years is a short time horizon to work with, from this question, we can clearly see what is on Katie and Roger's minds about their money. Like most who are in their 20s to 40s, they're in a period of transition and trying to juggle debt, savings, careers, and growing a family.

The "What do you want to see happen in three years?" question helps to initiate a brainstorming session about what you hope to accomplish in your life. The examples above serve as a big-picture overview of what our couple Katie and Roger are looking to accomplish. From there, it's time to make these goals S.M.A.R.T.

HOW S.M.A.R.T. ARE YOUR GOALS?

When it comes to your personal and financial life, making your goals as concrete as possible will help you focus on what's really important. A goal that's well-defined will be easier to visualize and easier to stick with.

S.M.A.R.T. goals are:
- Specific
- Measurable
- Attainable
- Relevant
- Timely

Specific: Be as detailed as possible. Think about the who, what, when and why involved. "I want to save $45,000 for a down payment on a home in the next four years" is a goal that answers "How much?" "How long?" and "What for?"

> *Katie and Roger would actually like to buy a home in the next 18 months and will need $20,000 at that time for a down payment.*

Measurable: You should be able to track your progress, so set milestones you want to achieve throughout your goal timeline. How close are you to meeting your goal? How much more do you need to save?

> *In order to have $20,000 in 18 months saved for a down payment, Katie and Roger will need to put away $1,111 per month.*

Attainable: You don't want to "shoot for the stars" and end up disappointed. Make sure you're setting goals that are realistic. Maxing out your 401(k) contribution, planning a European vacation, starting your own business, or building up a sufficient emergency savings are good places to start.

> *Can Katie and Roger find an additional $1,111 per month to save and still live comfortably? Chances are that since they want to pay off debt and build up their emergency fund, they will need to adjust this goal and timeline.*

Relevant: Choose a goal that aligns with your values and is relevant to your life and meaningful to you. Your goals should reflect yours and your family's needs, values and desires. If you're not thrilled about the prospect of owning a home, for example, then maybe it's not the right goal for you.

> *Katie and Roger indicated that purchasing a home would make them feel more comfortable and settled with their family.*

Timely: Set deadlines for yourself to keep the motivation going. Ask yourself how long it will take you to accomplish your goal. Working within a time frame allows you to better track your progress.

While this is a priority for Katie and Roger, their bigger priorities are getting out of debt and cushioning their emergency fund. They're going to adjust this goal to seven years out and focus in on the other two first.

PRIORITIZATION IS KEY

When thinking about and setting your goals, ask yourself what would have to happen in the next three, five, ten years and beyond in order for you to be happy. From there, begin to prioritize. Think about which goals make you the most excited and motivated or which ones will have the most impact on your life. Remember to include both short-term and long-term goals in your plans. Ideally, you'll want to have at least three of each.

You are likely to have multiple goals across a plethora of categories, so it's important to remember that you can do it all; you just can't do it all at once. Pick two or three top goals to focus on initially. As you cross one goal off, rotate in the next one and so on. Hone in on the goals that matter most to you financially and emotionally in order to see the biggest impact on your financial happiness.

Money Move

Figuring out why money is important to you and the role you want it to play in your life is a great way to ensure you attach your values to your goals. The more aligned your goals are with the things that are truly important to you in life, the more likely you are to stick to a plan of attack in achieving them.

Take time to complete these Money Moves:

☐ Answer the question: "If we were sitting down three years from now, what would have had to happen personally, professionally and financially in order for you to be happy?"

☐ Use your answers to create three short- and long-term S.M.A.R.T. goals and prioritize which one or two to accomplish first.

☐ Select a date each month to review your financial goal progress and put it on the calendar.

☐ Once goals are created, quantified and prioritized, break them down into monthly savings allotments. For example, if you need to save $10,000 for a new car in three years, you'll need to stash away $278 per month over the next 36 months.

Chapter 2:

PUT YOUR MONEY WHERE YOUR HEART IS

"Balancing your money is the key to having enough."
~ Elizabeth Warren

If I've figured out anything in my career, it's the fact that it doesn't matter how much money you make or how old you are, the majority of people simply don't know where their money goes. Considering that only one in three Americans prepares a detailed household budget, it's no wonder that money is a top cause of stress in people's lives.[2]

Before we dig in further or your eyes glaze over at the traditional chapter on "budgeting," consider this:

There's a divide in the personal finance world. On one side you have the finger-wagging cohort that tells you to cut your lattes, bring your lunch to work, and start tracking your spending to the penny. On the other, you have the group who tells you not to budget at all! Instead, simply practice "conscious spending" and align your money

---

[2] http://www.gallup.com/poll/162872/one-three-americans-prepare-detailed-household-budget.aspx

with what's important to you. Once you do, the rest will take care of itself.

I don't care what you call it. Budgeting is budgeting no matter what trendy label is placed upon it, and it happens to be a very necessary step in your financial life. However, does it mean you need to cut your favorite Pilates class or limit your happy hours? If that's what's important to you, then probably not.

I've already said I'm not the latte-cutting type. What I *am*, however, is the cash-flow-tracking type. Whether you want to hear it or not, you've got to figure out where your money is currently going *before* you can direct it to the areas you targeted in Chapter 1. You have to control your money, and having a plan in place that incorporates "conscious spending" is the first step on your path to workable wealth. This allows you to track your income and expenses and direct your dollars to where you want them to go.

I recently had a consultation call with Ben and Kim, both age 34, who were earning $300,000 a year. They had two kids, owned a home they were renting out for an amount that just covered the mortgage, $321,000 in student loans, $20,000 in credit card debt, a leased car, and $5,000 in a savings account that was dwindling fast. They had no idea where their money was going or how to start figuring it out. That same week, I spoke with Sharon, age 28, who was earning $45,000 a year, had recently opened her own coaching company and was just about to hit $15,000 in credit card debt. She wasn't bringing in enough money to support her lifestyle and didn't know where to cut back.

It doesn't matter how much money you make or how much you have in the bank, not knowing where your money is going is a common problem across all ages and incomes.

It's one thing to think you're only spending $250 a month on dining out. It's another to see that you're *actually* dropping $600 in a period of just 30 days. When you take the time to dig into what you're truly spending versus what you "think" you're spending, chances are you're going to see some discrepancies. You'll see things you weren't aware of in your spending habits, and you may find that you spend a lot more in some areas than you thought. The top ten areas for spending discrepancies that I've found with clients are:

- Dining out
- Groceries
- Entertainment
- Travel
- Gifts
- Clothes
- Personal Care
- Bars & Alcohol
- Clothes
- Electronics

Having a spending plan enables you to target areas that don't mean that much to you so you can redirect those funds towards what matters most. Should you maintain the $100- per-month gym membership you don't use, or could that $100 go towards your home down payment? Knowing where your money is going will enable you to direct it towards the goals that are important to you like a new car, a laptop upgrade, annual vacations, building up an adequate emergency fund, or stashing $5,500 into your Roth IRA.

MAKE A MONEY PLAN THAT MAKES YOU HAPPY

I still remember opening my first checking account. Bank of America kindly took on a wide-eyed, 15-year-old customer and passed along a debit card, checkbook and registry. I *loved* keeping track of my checks and debits in that little book. The numbers made me happy, and I felt secure knowing what the balance was at all times (big or small). I'm still that way today and have an Excel version for our household checking account. But while I track what's coming in and out of the account on a dollar basis, it's still *so* hard to see where it's actually going using that method.

Thank goodness we live in a time when technology and systems are making our lives easier with each day. This means we have options when it comes to figuring out where our money is going. Remember, it's not about finding the one "right" way to handle your money. It's about understanding what works for *you*. Here are a few ideas to get you started:

Analyze Your Cash Flow

Your first step is to understand where you're at with expenses so you can map out a plan for where you want to go.

Option 1: Write down and categorize what you spend each day for a month. Total the items and categories after 30 days and target areas to adjust. Then add up the hours you spent doing this and feel bad that you didn't go for Option 2.

Option 2: Sign up for online software that will do the analyzing for you! My favorites are Mint, You Need a Budget, QuickBooks or Quicken. These sites will allow you to link up your credit cards, debit cards and checking accounts and get an up-to-date snapshot of different categories of your spending. Easy-peasy.

Once your spending is analyzed by one of the uber-efficient tools above, it should only take you an hour or so to build out a plan for yourself in terms of areas to maintain, where to eliminate or reduce, and what to add in. It's best to create a spending plan based on your monthly expenses so that you can obtain a comprehensive view of all of your bills. Additionally, this will allow you to monitor the areas in which you want to increase and decrease spending.

What's Coming In?

Chances are that figuring out what's coming *in* to your bank accounts is going to be your favorite part of this whole cash-flow-tracking exercise. Who doesn't like earning (and counting) money?

Your income is going to include items like: your salary, bonuses, business income, interest on any savings or investments, government benefits and so on. It may help to look at your pay stubs or last year's taxes to get clear on the exact amounts. For now, go with a "net" or "after-tax" amount when tracking your income. Whatever hits your account after taxes is fair game for spending and saving.

Since most of your expenses occur on a monthly basis, it's best to average your income out to what you can expect each month as well.

What's Going Out?

After listing out your income, it's time to track your expenses, which will be divided into two categories: fixed and discretionary.

Fixed expenses are those expenses that are steady, ongoing and non-negotiable, meaning you need to pay for them each month. This includes your rent or mortgage payment, car payments, insurance, student loans and utilities. Discretionary expenses are items that fluctuate in costs and in some cases are more optional than mandatory to pay for. These include items such as groceries, eating out, retail therapy, movies, salon outings, entertainment, gifts and vacations.

Keep in mind that not all expenses are created equal. This means that while some expenses may occur on a weekly or monthly basis, others are seasonal, like holiday gift expenses or an annual summer vacation. Others are occasional, like car repairs or a trip to the dentist. It may take some time with tracking your expenses to get a good idea of what you spend on an average monthly or yearly basis.

What if You're in the Red?

When looking at your fixed expenses, savings goals, and discretionary expenses subtracted from your average income for the same period, check out what number is left over. If it's positive, you're ahead of the game! This surplus can be converted into more savings or investments in reaching your goals.

If all you see is red, then it's time to make some bigger changes. Bottom line: You spend more than you make. The only way to put yourself back on the positive side is to either increase your income or decrease your expenses. (Check out Chapter 8 for ways to grow your income.) No matter what the number left over is, you still want to review how much money you spend and what you spend it on. With the numbers in front of you, it's time to answer these questions:

- What areas are you overspending in that you hadn't realized?

- What are the areas you targeted as being important to you to invest time or money into? What are you currently spending in these areas and what would you like to be spending?

- Are you only making the minimum payments on your credit cards and other consumer debt?

- Is there a line item for saving that includes emergency funds and retirement?

- Which areas are you going to cut back on to make room for bigger priorities? (This is the big one. If you truly want to make a change in your finances and take control of your money, you *need* to be willing to make adjustments to your spending. Sacrifices will be made, but they're being made for your overall peace of mind and happiness.)

Make Room

I'm not here to tell you to start tracking what you spend each year on bottled water and shampoo, because ultimately what you spend your money on is 150% up to *you*. Whether or not you reach your goals, get out of debt, are prepared for retirement, or take that annual trip to the Caribbean are also up to you. If you want to feel good about where your money is going, make sure you have these areas covered when looking at your cash flow:

Debt Repayment: If you only pay the minimum due on your credit cards, see if you can make room to double the payment on the one with the highest interest rate.

Emergency Savings: If you're one of the six in ten Americans who doesn't have enough cash to handle unexpected expenses, then it's time to build your emergency fund.[3] Set a goal of building that first $1,000 and then increase from there.

Retirement Savings: If you're not sure how much you should be saving, aim to stash away 10% of your income if you're under age 30. Aim for 15% if you're over 30. If you can handle more than these amounts, do it! (We'll check out the power of compound interest and how it works wonders for you in Chapter 6.)

S.M.A.R.T. Goals: If you know what you want to focus on, make sure your goals have a line item in your budget. Include your top two or three goals from Chapter 1 (if they're not covered above). Although the numbers will say to knock out all of your debt before you start saving, I believe that you can and should work towards more than one financial goal at once. If you're in debt but don't have an emergency fund in place, what happens when the car breaks down or a pet gets sick? You'll throw those expenses right back on a credit card and undo any work you've done to pay off balances. By stashing $50 or $100 a month into an emergency fund while also working to wipe out your debt, you can protect yourself against some of the unknown.

KEEP THINGS SEPARATE

One of the biggest cash flow issues I see are the occasional expenses that will derail a budget. If you're someone who is always searching

---

[3] http://www.bankrate.com/finance/smart-spending/money-pulse-0115.aspx

for cash for the holidays, playing catch up when your insurance premium hits, scraping to pay for your best friend's wedding events, or waiting to buy plane tickets to visit family until your bonus hits, then it's time to get yourself organized! You're never going to get your finances on track if you let these expenses derail you each time.

If you know there's a big expense coming up, open a separate savings account for it and work the savings into your monthly budget. This allows you to save for the expense ahead of time and keeps you from stressing out when it arrives. Here's how it can work in your life:

Katrina loves to travel. Cross-country visits to see family, annual trips to Europe, and cruises around Mexico – she wants to do it all. When we met, she was putting these trips on her credit cards and then paying off the balances over time. After doing some planning work, we set an annual travel budget of $4,800 for Katrina and broke it down into a $400-per-month savings goal. Katrina opened a separate savings account for this goal; and when it came time to book trips, she used the money she had available. If she didn't have enough to cover a trip, she wouldn't take it. Setting the limit and allocating a separate account helped to ensure she was using her money to pursue her desire of traveling without breaking the bank.

Depending on your goals, you might consider opening saving accounts for things like:

- Travel
- Insurance Premiums (Car, Home, Rental)
- Charitable Giving
- Home Maintenance
- Holiday Expenses
- Home Down Payment
- Wedding
- Going Back to School or Educational Programs

KEEP YOURSELF ON TRACK

Keeping yourself in line and on track with a new plan can be hard to do. Enlist some help and consider the tips below when organizing your spending.

Follow the 90% Principle

It doesn't matter if it's financial or physical, there are a ton of things that we *want* in life. Whether it's a vacation, a new car, that sugary milkshake, or the bowl of mac-n-cheese, moderation is key. My friend, Amy Clover, says she teaches her clients the "90% Principle." Amy founded Strong Inside Out, a site that empowers people to rise out of struggle with fitness and into a positive mindset. Following her principle means that 90% of the time, you eat healthy. She says the other 10% should be reserved for those things you just can't do without, because completely knocking out the foods you enjoy and depriving yourself could backfire.

It's hard to make a clean cut when breaking any habit, and spending money is no exception. Instead of limiting yourself by cutting out your daily Starbucks run altogether or swearing that you'll stop hitting up happy hours with friends or dining out, turn these events into celebrations so you can still partake when you hit small financial goals. Or try setting a monthly cap that you agree not to go over. It could be $50, $100 or $200, but whatever it is, practice self-control and simply do not budge on the ceiling you set.

Get an Accountability Buddy

Two is better than one when it comes to staying motivated. Enlist a significant other, friend, business partner, or family member to hold you accountable in reaching your goals and staying on track. Set weekly money dates for yourself to review progress and target areas for cutbacks and improvements. (More on Money Dates in Chapter 10.)

Be Real with Yourself

Are you the kind of person who will decide to get up at 5:00 am every day and spring out of bed ready to go, or do you need four hits of the snooze button and a wake-up call from your mom to make it happen? Be real with how much structure you need in place to stay on track and implement one of the following:

The Cash Envelope Method: If you need to be super restrictive with yourself, go for this method. Withdraw the limit you've set for a weekly or bi-weekly period from the ATM for items like shopping, groceries or dining out. Put the cash into a separate envelope for each category. When you're out of cash in the envelope for a category, that's it. You're out until your next pay period. If you're truly in a bind (for example, if you need groceries), you may decide to pull from another envelope or category for spending if you're willing to make the sacrifice in that area.

Keep a Ledger: My husband and I have taken to sharing a note labeled "Spending" in the Reminders app on our iPhones. We have a set amount for discretionary spending at the beginning of every two-week period; and then as we each hit the grocery store, get gas, grab lunch, or make a wine or coffee run, we'll deduct it from the amount. This way at any point in time we can both see what we have left to spend for the period. (This also forces us to plan ahead for birthdays, group dinners, wedding gifts, and so on.)

Set an Alert: If you're pretty confident in your spending and just want a few gentle reminders when you're treading close to limits, you may want to use Mint's budgeting feature. The feature allows you to enter spending limits for specific categories. If you get close to or surpass the limit, Mint will send you a polite email telling you to please get your life in order. Or it will just call you out when you're about to or have overspent. I for one love the wake-up emails.

Set a Dollar Limit for Impulse Purchases

Impulse spending is the quickest way to derail your financial plan. Set a limit of $100 (or whatever works for your situation) and follow the protocol that anything over that amount should require a 24-hour waiting period before buying. The 24-hour time period should be spent determining the answers to the following questions:

- What are you planning on giving up to purchase this item? Dining out? Your personal trainer for the month? Where will you make up the difference?

- How will you feel *after* purchasing the item? Excited for the new buy, or guilty when you look at your bank or credit card statement?

- What does this item represent for you? Will you feel better looking? Wealthier? More tech-savvy? What problem will this product solve and can it be solved with tools you have on hand?

Impulse spending feels exciting, but it can often cause the most harm to a financial plan. This is because they're expenses that aren't planned for and the resources for the purchase are borrowed using credit cards or pulled from another priority. Either way, you end up behind somewhere.

Understand "Wants" and "Needs"

We all have basic needs that we must take care of, but beyond that it's easy to blur the line between want versus need. It's natural to feel like you "need" or "deserve" something after working hard all week or month long, but it's important to understand the items that take precedence.

Get Clear on Priorities

Do you even really want that thing you're trying to buy but can't afford? As famous actor and writer Will Rogers said, "Too many people spend money they haven't earned, to buy things they don't want, to impress people they don't like."

Stop buying things you can't afford and aren't in line with your true priorities anyway! The trouble typically comes when you spend money to reward yourself with items that you don't really need. Sometimes, if you're honest with yourself, you'll discover that you don't really *want* those items, either. Prioritize what you value, not what society or friends and family say should be important.

Saving a pre-set amount each month and understanding fixed and discretionary expenses first should allow for adjustments to be made and a plan to be put in place if there is an item that you truly want. The key is to know that the latest version of the iPhone or upgraded television is likely a want and not a need.

When You Need to Make a Change

Identify where your wants are in your budget. The problem isn't the cost of your lattes, daily lunches, weekly happy hours, or yoga classes. It's the lack of awareness in what's being spent in each area. If there's room for it all in your spending plan and you can still take care of your goals for yourself in the present and future, then keep at it! However, if there's need for change, which area are you willing to cut back on? Identify what you're willing to reduce or eliminate from your wants to allocate towards higher priorities and even evaluate things you think of as needs.

Do you have a gym membership you don't use? Can you reduce your phone bill by switching providers? Can you remember to turn off lights and appliances to reduce your utility bills? What about price shopping your car or homeowner's insurance? If you have $1,000 in your emergency fund, increasing your deductible to $1,000 could add money back into your cash flow. One of the best ways to save is to lower your monthly recurring expenses.

Pay Yourself First

Make a commitment to contribute to your company's 401(k) plan, build your emergency fund, or max out your Roth IRA for the year. Break these big achievements down into monthly goals. Automatically deduct the amounts from your paycheck or set up an automatic transfer from your checking account. Automating will allow you to treat your savings like a bill payment and anything left over will be yours to spend and work with.

A SHOUT OUT TO THOSE WITH VARIABLE INCOMES

If you're an entrepreneur, freelancer, or employed in a profession that comes with a variable income, you don't have the luxury of pulling in the same amount of money on a bi-weekly or monthly basis. While not knowing exactly what your monthly income will look like makes managing finances more difficult, it's not impossible.

Having a volatile, variable income underlines the importance of tracking *all* your cash flow. Budgets need to be as flexible as your income and you'll want to create a spending plan that easily shows what items can be cut or eliminated if funds are low one month. For example, using detailed "meals out" and "entertainment" categories as part of your spending plan will help you to easily and painlessly eliminate these two budget areas if you experience a leaner month. In this way, you can make sure the smaller amount of cash coming in is allocated to your real needs, like bills, utilities and groceries.

Accept a Slightly Leaner Lifestyle

When you're on a variable income, you need to be particularly careful to guard against lifestyle inflation. Your income may allow you to live large one month, but the next month could see a slow-down and a subsequent painful drop in earnings. Streamline your expenses so you consistently have the same outflows month-over-month. When those big income months do occur, you'll simply have more left over to put towards savings goals, instead of using it as an opportunity to splurge.

Multiple Fallbacks

Although everyone should have money set aside for emergencies, having a variable income makes it important to create *multiple* fallback funds. You're at a higher risk of coming up short when you need money to cover something unforeseen because your income varies. Aim to set aside three to six months' worth of household expenses that can help you get by if you experience a few months of low earnings. Once you have this fund established, work to build a separate fund that will help cover emergency situations.

In addition to a comfortable cushion for emergencies and low-income months, you also need a cushion for your future. Entrepreneurs need to be diligent about saving for retirement as there aren't any employers looking over your shoulder to offer you sponsored plans or company matches. As an entrepreneur, you have a lot of great options, like a SEP IRA, Solo 401(k) or a Simple IRA. (More on this in Chapter 6). Don't forget to factor these into your cash flow.

Don't Slack – You Can Still Automate

Take a look at your past earnings on an annual and monthly basis and calculate an average. Knowing what you are likely to bring in versus what your expected expenses are will allow you to make a pretty safe guess about what you can contribute to savings each month. Set up an automated payment to your accounts, because it's easy to forget or let it slide if you have to do it manually every time. Because your income *will* change, adjustments will be necessary over time but starting small with a conservative number will give you the automated foundation to work from.

GOING FORWARD WITH YOUR NEW BUDGET

Economists at Princeton and New York University estimate that around one-third of all US households live paycheck to paycheck.[4] If you're tired of feeling stressed and anxious about your money, then it's time to stop ignoring it. Break the "shiny object" syndrome, cut back in the areas that aren't that important to you, and be willing to do the work to avoid a money mess and develop the life you want to have.

Changes are necessary, but remember the benefits of taking action. By gaining control of your finances, you'll be able to:

- Pay off debts to reduce your monthly obligations

- Build an emergency fund to protect your family from disaster

- Save for large purchases like a vacation, a car or a house

- Invest for a comfortable retirement

By taking the above steps and beginning to document and become aware of your spending patterns, you'll automatically feel more confident about your situation and any plan you put in place to move yourself forward. From there, each adjustment that you make will put you even closer to financial freedom.

---

4   http://www.brookings.edu/about/projects/bpea/papers/2014/wealthy-hand-to-mouth

Money Move

It's time to put your money where your heart is. Take time to analyze where it's currently going and target areas for improvement. From there you can reduce or eliminate unnecessary items for those that take higher priority.

Take time now to complete these Money Moves and align your spending with your values:

☐ Sync up your credit cards, checking accounts and debit cards on the platform of your choosing and begin to analyze where your money is going.

☐ Gather information on income and expenses.

☐ Sit down and create a spending plan for yourself. Target areas to cut back in, if needed, and ensure you're making adjustments to realign funds with categories that are most important to you.

☐ Review the budget you created and ensure it includes the items below. If it doesn't, return to the step above and make further adjustments.

- Emergency Savings
- Retirement Savings
- Debt Pay Down
- Two or three of your goals from Chapter 1

☐ Decide if you'll follow the envelope, ledger, alert, or accountability system to stay on track with your spending. Take the next hour to get yourself set up for the first two weeks.

- ☐ Set up separate savings accounts for the expenses that can "derail" your budget. Break the expenses into monthly savings amounts to factor into your cash flow and automate your savings.

- ☐ Set a limit for impulse purchases and stick to it!

- ☐ Schedule a recurring appointment on your calendar to review your cash flow on a weekly basis. After three months, adjust to every two weeks; and after six months, if you're comfortable, move to monthly check-ins.

Chapter 3:

GET CREDIT SAVVY

"Don't tell me where your priorities are. Show me where you spend your money and I'll tell you what they are." ~ James W. Frick

I've said it before and I'll probably say it again: Your credit score is one of the most important numbers in your life. This three-digit number essentially acts as your financial report card, except there's no leaving it behind after graduation. Your credit score is used to represent your creditworthiness, which translates into the likelihood that you'll pay your debts in a timely manner.

If managed wisely, it can bring you peace of mind and result in dollars in your pocket via low interest rates and higher credit limits. If not managed properly, your credit score can delay your ability to reach goals and result in you spending more money than necessary to make up for past mistakes.

HOW CAN YOUR CREDIT SCORE IMPACT YOUR OVERALL FINANCES?

Check out this example for how a positive score can translate into thousands of dollars saved:

Claire maintains good financial habits. She pays her credit cards off in full each month, has set her bills to automatically draft out of her checking account so she never misses a payment, and has a positive credit history that dates back ten years. She's in the market to buy a home and got approved for a $200,000, 30-year fixed-rate mortgage at a 3.75% interest rate.

Steve, on the other hand, has a murky history with his credit. He got his first credit card at age 18 and ran up some debt during college that took him a while to conquer. He doesn't have the best system in place for keeping track of his bills and gets hit with the occasional late and bounced check fees. He's finally getting himself organized and has cut his credit card debt in half, but still carries ongoing balances and has at least one old account in collections. Steve's in the market for a new home, too, and was approved for the same $200,000, 30-year fixed-rate mortgage. But with his credit history, the best interest rate he could secure was 5.5%.

Claire's credit score and solid financial history earned her a good interest rate on her mortgage. Over the life of her loan, she'll pay $133,443.23 in interest.

Steve's not-so-good credit history landed him a higher-than-ideal interest rate, but his credit wasn't so bad that he didn't get approved for the loan. His interest rate was 1.75% higher than Claire's, which seems like a small difference, but Steve will pay $208,808.08 in interest over the life of his loan.

That "small" increase in interest will cost Steve an extra $75,364.85! Steve may have wonderful habits today, but because his credit history and score reflect some of the poor behaviors he had in the past, he'll now be spending much more money than Claire to make up for it. I don't know about you, but I could do *a lot* with an extra $75,000!

This example of the interest rate differential will apply throughout your financial life. Home loans, car loans, and credit cards will all cost you more if you don't have your financial habits on point.

WHAT'S A FICO, ANYWAY?

FICO is a software company founded in 1956 by Bill Fair and Earl Isaac. The company was established as Fair, Isaac and Company, changed to Fair Isaac Corporation in 2003, and then rebranded to FICO in 2009.

The FICO score was created as a measure of consumer credit risk and is used by banks and credit grantors in the United States, Mexico, and Canada. The score is based upon your consumer credit files within three national credit bureaus: Experian, Equifax, and Transunion.

WHAT MAKES UP YOUR SCORE?

When it comes to your credit score, not all items are treated equally. There are five elements that make up your FICO credit score:

- 35% of your score is based on how you pay your bills. If you always make payments on time, this will positively impact your score. If you're often late or have bankruptcies, liens, or repossessions, that could hurt you.

- 30% of your score is based on the amount of money you owe and the amount of available credit to you. This goes beyond your credit utilization ratio. This category also takes into account the number of accounts with balances, the types of accounts with balances, the amounts owed on installment loans, and how much revolving credit is being used.

- 15% is based on the length of your credit history. The longer your credit history, the more positive the impact on your score. The age of your oldest account and the average age of all of your credit accounts are factored in here.

- 10% is based on the mix of your credit accounts. This involves both revolving credit, such as credit cards, and installment credit, such as mortgages and car loans.

- The final 10% is based on new credit applications. This takes into account how many new accounts and the number of recent inquiries you have, the length of time since credit report inquiries were made and how long it's been since you've opened a new account.

There's a common misconception that applying for new credit will reduce your FICO score. Your credit score allows for "rate shopping." If you're getting multiple inquiries from mortgage or auto dealers over a short period, these are usually treated as one inquiry and have minimal impact on your score. But if you're shopping for multiple credit cards in a short period, this can reflect as higher risk and ding your score.

FICO Score Range

Your FICO score will range from 300-850 and the higher the number, the better. The breakdown of credit score ranges can vary, but this is a good overview:

- 720-850: Excellent
- 690-719: Good credit
- 630-689: Fair (average) credit
- 580- 630: Poor credit
- <580: Bad Credit

ENSURE YOUR REPORT AND SCORE ARE ACCURATE

Use a website such as annualcreditreport.com or Credit Karma to obtain your credit report and look for discrepancies at least once a year. You can access your score with Credit Karma or at credit.com. If you find anything amiss, you should immediately contact both the credit reporting agency and the company that is portraying inaccurate information. There will likely be phone calls, letters and emails involved to get it updated. It may be a headache, but your credit score is compiled from the information found on your credit report. If your report is inaccurate, those errors could reflect on your score and cause it to be lower than it should be, which can cost you money.

HOW TO MAINTAIN A HIGH SCORE

Taking the following actions – consistently and over time will help you maintain a high credit score.

Be responsible. How you pay your bills accounts for 35% of your score, which makes it essential to pay your bills on time. If you're late on a consistent basis or have been sent to collections, that can hurt your score. This doesn't just apply to credit card accounts. It also takes into account utilities, retail accounts, installment loans, finance company accounts, and mortgages. Note that how recent and the frequency of late payments matters.

Carry a low or zero balance. Having maxed-out cards translates into a low amount of available credit (meaning lenders think you need to borrow funds to live day to day or aren't tracking your spending closely). When you're perceived as overextended, it translates into a higher risk credit score.

Avoid closing accounts (for the most part). Closing credit card accounts that have a zero balance and are in good standing will not raise your credit score. This can impact your average credit history and effectively reduces the amount of credit available to you, which can increase your credit utilization ratio, and actually lower your score.

Start building your credit now. The longer you've had a responsible credit history, the higher your score.

Be proactive. If there's an issue that you foresee, such as being late on a payment, a bounced check or anything else of the matter, reach out to the company or creditor to give them a heads up. You'll likely establish higher rapport and will prevent them from having to track you down. You may even be able to get any fees associated with the mishap waived.

WHAT YOU SHOULD KNOW ABOUT YOUR CREDIT CARDS

Did you know that the average adult in the US has a total of $5,596 in consumer debt?[5] It's easy to see from that statistic alone why credit cards get a bad rap. If you're not careful, it's pretty clear that credit cards can wreak havoc on your finances in a variety of ways.

If not managed wisely, you could rack up so much debt that it will take years to pay off, resulting in thousands of dollars in interest being paid by you. Not only could this damage your credit score in the process, but it also means all of that money is being taken away from your other financial goals and things you'd like to accomplish. Talk about a spiral!

But here's the thing: Credit cards don't have to be bad. Using a credit card doesn't mean an automatic road to bad consumer debt. Credit, just like money, is a tool. Used right, it can help you purchase things you need or set goals for (such as a house or a reliable car), but you have to start smart and educate yourself about them before you use them.

USE YOUR CREDIT CARDS THE FINANCIALLY WISE WAY

Credit cards do not equal free money. You're borrowing money from someone else, someone who can and will track you down if you don't pay them back. Not in the scary Mafia sense, but in the sense of, we're going to keep tacking on penalties and interest until you want to hide in a corner and wish you never took the

---

[5] http://www.creditcards.com/credit-card-news/credit-card-debt-statistics-1276.php

borrowed money to begin with. Any type of credit available to you is borrowed money; and before you borrow it, you better have a plan for paying it back.

You might want to treat your credit card like a debit card. Don't charge more than you can afford (no matter what your credit limit is), and be mindful of how much you have in your bank account so you don't end up in a situation where you can't afford to pay your balance. Purchase only what you need and use the card only for routine or planned purchases within your budget. You want to be able to pay your credit card off in full every month, and you should. Keeping a low balance is also a good idea. If you have a credit limit of $5,000, that doesn't mean you should have a balance of $4,500 at the end of the month, even if you can afford it. With how much you owe factored into your credit score, keeping a low balance will reflect positively on your score.

Understanding APRs and Fees

One of the most important things you should understand is the annual percentage rate, or APR, on your credit card. If you fail to pay your balance in full, you'll be charged the APR on all or part of your remaining balance. This means what you originally purchased for $20 might end up costing you $25 next month and increase from there.

To translate this into your life, if your credit card carries a rate of 20%, you'll pay $20 for every $100 you charge. So if you're carrying $10,000 in credit card debt, you're looking at $2,000 per year in interest! Ask yourself, is all of that stuff worth an extra $2,000 over what you paid for it? Would you buy it in the first place knowing it will end up costing you that much more? This is why paying your balance off in full every month is critical.

When shopping for the best credit card for you, check out websites like Nerdwallet or CreditCards.com for a comparison of the best cards and offers available. Keep in mind that while you want the lowest APR available, beware of promotional offers. Some cards have low introductory rates for just a year and then increase substantially thereafter.

Be wary of fees as well. A number of credit cards, especially those that promise rewards or points, have annual fees. This fee will be charged during your first billing cycle, although some products will waive the fee for the first year and start charging it in the second year. Read the fine print before signing up for a credit card if you want one without an annual fee. Late fees also apply if you fail to make a payment within a certain time period (usually 21 days). If you've previously made timely payments, you may be able to get a late fee waived, but don't count on it. Late fees are capped at $25 for first-time offenders and $35 for frequent offenders under the Credit Card Act of 2009.

What's Up With Minimum Payments?

Take a look at your monthly credit card statement. You should notice a section that tells you the minimum payment you can make. While these payments are designed to look manageable in comparison with your balances, be sure to factor in interest. Your statement should have a box that tells you how long it will take to pay off your balance if you only pay the minimum due and compare it to how long it would take if you made a higher payment. This box will also state the total dollar amount you can expect to pay in interest when making these payments. This could be pretty shocking when you thought those new shoes were only going to cost you $80 but you now owe $140.

Any time you leave a portion of your balance unpaid, interest will accrue on that balance. If you continue making charges on your card while paying the minimum owed, you won't be able to catch up to paying your balance off.

What About Rewards

When you make purchases with a rewards card, you acquire points to redeem for travel, cash back, and other goods. Sounds kind of awesome, right? It's awesome only if you play the game how we've just discussed. You can't charge everything you want to the card just to get the points and then be stuck with a high, interest-accruing balance.

Credit card companies don't offer these rewards programs out of the kindness of their hearts. They offer them because they're smart and fully expect people to use credit irresponsibly. The majority of people will end up having to pay interest on their balances, and the money that they thought was a free bonus ends up not being free after all. This means the credit card companies win and they earn a profit off the interest rates charged to those who don't (or can't) pay off balances.

Rewards cards and the points you can "earn" only benefit you if you limit yourself to everyday spending you already planned for. The moment you start charging extras to your card in an effort to grab more points is the moment that rewards cards become a threat to your financial situation.

The Upside of Credit Cards

Credit cards aren't all bad. They actually come with many safety features that you won't get with other forms of payment like cash or debit cards. When you charge something on your credit card, it doesn't immediately deduct anything from your checking account and you're not out any cash until you pay that credit card bill.

This is a good thing in terms of guarding against fraudulent activity and mistakes on your statement. If you paid with cash, you may or may not get that money back. You can always dispute a charge on your credit card. Remember, paying with a debit card is similar to cash and the money in your account is taken out as soon as that transaction posts. If you're a victim of fraud or want to dispute the charge, you may or may not get that money back.

SHOULD YOU USE YOUR CREDIT CARDS?

There's a divide when it comes to this answer. Many people are staunchly against using credit when you could stick with your debit cards or use only cash. Their case is pretty solid. If you can't manage your finances or control your spending, your credit cards can fast track you into financial disaster. But while that's a possibility, it isn't the rule. There are many advantages and reasons why others prefer using credit over debit or cash.

As with many personal finance issues, there may not be one right answer as to whether or not you should use credit cards. If you're struggling to develop good money habits and juggling credit card balances now, it's probably smart to stick to cash or debit until you can better manage your money. (Check out Chapter 4 for strategies and guidelines on tackling your debt.) However, if you're educated on how your cards work, use them responsibly, pay them off in full each month, and you already keep a budget and track all your spending, then a credit card can be a useful tool in your financial toolbox with some perks you can cash in on every so often along the way.

Money Move

Just like your spending plan and your goals, your credit is a tool to use with your money. It can be incredibly helpful and add a ton of value in tackling financial goals and projects along the way, or it can be an impediment to you making much progress.

Take time to complete these Money Moves:

☐ Head to annualcreditreport.com to pull your credit and consider signing up for Credit Karma.

☐ Once you have your credit report in hand, schedule one hour to review the information, noting any discrepancies or negative information.

☐ After reviewing your credit report, you should understand:
- The list of accounts being reported on
- If there is any fraudulent activity
- What your credit score looks like
- The factors listed as helping or hurting your score
- If you need to take action on any balances or reported information

☐ Now that you have the necessary information, create a plan of action for improving your score, if needed. This may include:

- Contacting creditors about delinquent accounts
- Paying more than the minimum on outstanding balances
- Obtaining a secured card to learn how to use credit responsibly and begin build a credit history.

Chapter 4:

KICK YOUR DEBT TO THE CURB

"Too many people spend money they haven't earned, to buy things they don't want, to impress people that they don't like." ~ Will Rogers

Even with a degree and a career in personal finance, I've made my share of financial mistakes. I've always been financially conscious, but my younger self is guilty of letting items slip by on the money front. (Thank goodness for overdraft protection!) Luckily, I recovered from my financial fumbles without major consequences, but I'll never forget how anxious and disappointed I felt in myself when I realized I'd messed up.

I see a lot of people making their own financial missteps in my line of work, and they often find themselves in debt as a consequence. Whether it's spending freely without resolve, only making the minimum payment due on cards, throwing a little bit extra towards each balance without a plan for truly tackling it, or trying to cut corners with zero-interest balance transfers only to have the time period expire and face a higher interest rate on the other side, the mistakes people make in acquiring and facing their debt can derail an entire financial plan.

How do you bounce back from a debt load that you feel like you can't shake off? When you've racked up debt across multiple loans, being free from it all seems like a distant dream. But it *is* possible to kick your debt to the curb! The first step is to get up close and personal with your debt. The second is to create a repayment plan that will work for you.

GET TO KNOW YOUR DEBT

If I asked you what the interest rate is on your credit card(s), would you be able to tell me without checking? Chances are you wouldn't – and you're not alone. I've had countless consultations and emails that ask how to go about best tackling a mountain of debt. When I ask about the interest rates and minimum payments due, the response is often another round of that uncomfortable silence I've talked about in previous chapters.

The Three Things You Must Know

If you want to tackle your debt, you must start by educating yourself about your own situation. Without the information below, you won't be able to put together an effective plan for knocking out balances. You need to know these three things:

1. Balances owed
2. Interest rates on each balance
3. Minimum payments due

It's time to roll up your sleeves and do some research so you can figure out what your total debt balance is across credit cards, auto loans, student loans, personal loans, mortgages, and more.

THE DIFFERENCE BETWEEN GOOD DEBT AND BAD DEBT

Before continuing the conversation on debt, it's important to understand that not all debt is created equal. Taking on debt can sometimes allow you to leverage your money to create opportunities and potential for a better financial future, but that's not always the case. It helps to know the differences between "bad" debt and "good" debt.

Bad debts are those that carry an *increasing* balance on an item of *decreasing* value. This includes auto loans and consumer credit card debt (which is usually accumulated with purchases on clothing, dining out, electronics, and other personal objects). These are items that lose value once you purchase them. On top of borrowing money from your auto financing or credit card company to buy these items, you're paying interest on the borrowed funds. This means your purchase is costing you more than if you had just paid cash.

Good debts are those where you used the principal funds to pay for something that will either increase in value or will provide a benefit, which can lead to increased earnings or value. Typically, good debts come with lower interest rates, too. While there are no guarantees, good debts generally include student loans and mortgage balances. Your student loans provide funding for your education, which in turn allows you to (theoretically) earn a higher income. Your mortgage provides you the ability to purchase a house, which may increase in value over time and result in you having a position with positive equity.

IDENTIFYING DEBT PROBLEM-CAUSERS

Chances are your debt – good, bad, or otherwise – didn't just show up at your doorstep one day by surprise. Whether you want to hear it or not, you likely had an active role in getting yourself into whatever debt situation you may or may not be in. While dwelling on the past is not something I'm a fan of, I do think it's important to understand past behaviors and changes that are needed in order to forge a better path ahead.

Identify some of your problem-causers and understand the role they may play in your spending. Some common problem-causers include:

- **_Eating Meals Out:_** Breakfast, Lunches, Snacks, Dinners, Happy Hours
- **_Habits:_** Coffee, Alcohol, Massages, Clothing
- **_Impulse Purchases:_** New iPhone is out? Boom! Purchased. Look at those boots. Added to the wardrobe! Set a limit on the impulse buying.
- **_Hobbies:_** Pilates Classes, Yoga, Crafts, Brewing Beer, Movies

These items add up! Consider the following $8.00 lunchtime example:

- $8 lunch x 5 days x 50 weeks = $2,000 per year
- $8 lunch x 3 days x 50 weeks = $1,200 per year
- $8 lunch x 2 days x 50 weeks = $800 a year

Now if you're perfectly happy spending $2,000 per year on lunches out because one of your goals is to have that kind of flexibility _and_ you're not incurring debt to make it happen, then great!

But if you're dining out and racking up the credit card debt, that's $2,000 that is accruing interest over time and setting you back from the things that are truly important to you. Could that money go towards helping you get closer to what you value, such as getting a lower-paying job with more life balance, pursuing more travel, or building a better wardrobe so you feel comfortable in your clothes? Again, the point is to be aware of where your money is going. The _what_ really doesn't matter as long as it's in line with your priorities and not causing financial trouble.

TIPS FOR GETTING YOUR SPENDING UNDER CONTROL

If you find yourself struggling to live within – and preferably beneath – your means, and know that your debt is getting out of control, consider these actions for reigning in your spending and taking control of your cash flow.

Get Creative: Make a game of ways to save money. What can you give up or cut back on for a short period of time? Set a goal of 30 or 60 days. You may find that you really don't need that expense.

Reduce Temptation: Leave your credit cards at home and stay out of stores that lure you to spend. Select a special item and set a goal to save for it instead of buying it impulsively.

Make Lifestyle Adjustments: Look into cutting out cable, start shopping with a list that you have to stick to, and forgo the movie theater and rent a movie or use Netflix. Consider carpooling, purchasing used instead of new, and setting caps on monthly spending in your "fun times" areas.

CREATE A REPAYMENT PLAN THAT WORKS

There are many ways to get out of debt, but the two most effective methods are the debt snowball and the debt avalanche. Both plans involve aggressively paying down one balance while making the minimum payments on the rest. The difference lies in what order you tackle the debts.

The Debt Snowball

Remember those Saturday morning cartoons where a character stands at the top of a snowy hill and sets a small snowball rolling down the slope? As the ball rolls, it picks up more snow, getting larger and larger (and moving with more speed) the further it travels downhill, until it eventually runs over another character or two along the way.

You can create that same snowball effect in your debt repayment. You start small and get bigger. With the debt snowball, you pay off your debt from the smallest to the largest balance. Financial radio show host Dave Ramsey has advocated this method for years.

Imagine you have the following debts:

1. Credit Card 1: $500 at 3.9% ($25 minimum payment)
2. Credit Card 2: $1,000 at 8% ($50 minimum payment)
3. Credit Card 3: $3,000 at 21.99% ($100 minimum payment)
4. Credit Card 4: $12,000 at 18.9% ($200 minimum payment)

Suppose you cut your expenses and have an extra $300 each month in your budget. By allocating this money entirely towards the lowest balance, you pay off your first loan in less than two months.

Once you eliminate the first debt, you free up the minimum payment. Your debt snowball is now $25 larger. You can now put $325 per month towards that second debt, in addition to the $50 minimum payment you're already making. You're now putting $375 per month towards that balance. You can pay it off in three months, and the debt snowball grows again.

The Benefits of the Debt Snowball

With the debt snowball, the focus is on motivating good habits. By concentrating on the smallest balances, you get a small win right at the beginning of the journey and quickly build a succession of wins. The excitement that comes from knocking out full balance after full balance helps you stay motivated and on course to dump all of your debt.

The Shortcomings of the Debt Snowball

Since the debt snowball focuses on balances instead of interest rates, there's the possibility that you'll end up spending more money and time tackling your debt. This is because you may not tackle the largest interest rate card right away, as it might not be the one with the smallest balance. Because of this small inefficiency, it may take you a few additional months to wipe out your balances with the debt snowball than with the debt avalanche.

If you can't stand the thought of paying extra interest, and you want to go the most mathematically optimal route, then the debt avalanche might work better for you.

The Debt Avalanche

The avalanche approach isn't, unfortunately, the sudden and unexpected obliteration of all your debts. Avalanche payments are about making the biggest long-term impact. So instead of focusing all of your extra debt-paying funds on the account with the lowest balance, you focus on the account with the highest interest rate.

With the debt avalanche, you pay the debts down from the highest interest rate to lowest interest rate. Here's what that list of debts from the previous page looks like if you use this method:

1. Credit Card 1: $3,000 at 21.99% ($100 minimum payment)
2. Credit Card 2: $12,000 at 18.9% ($200 payment)
3. Credit Card 3: $1,000 at 8% ($50 payment)
4. Credit Card 4: $500 at 3.9% ($25 payment)

Notice which debt is first now. If you send the same extra $300 to the $3,000 loan with the 21.99% interest rate first, paying off the first card takes eight months, instead of two (because of the larger balance). After you roll in the extra amount from paying off the first card, the second card takes 24 months.

Although it takes longer to knock out the initial balances, over time you'll pay less towards your debt because you eliminate the most costly interest rates immediately. The math often makes much more sense with the debt avalanche, but it does take more discipline because it takes longer to see big results.

The Benefits of the Debt Avalanche

With the debt avalanche method you pay less in interest, saving yourself money. If you have a large debt with a high interest rate, this strategy can save you a substantial sum (that can then be used towards other goals). Also, if you have two loans that are just about the same balance, you might as well tackle the higher interest rate first.

The Shortcomings of the Debt Avalanche

With the debt avalanche, it often takes a bit longer to pay off the first debt. In the example above, it takes six additional months to eliminate a payment on the first balance and the second credit card takes a total of 24 months; including the six months of minimum payments before you get the extra amount rolled in from paying off card one. If the long slog is discouraging, the debt snowball might help you stay motivated to complete the journey.

TACKLE YOUR DEBT

Ultimately, you have to weigh your goals against your own reasonable expectations for yourself. The avalanche approach will likely save you more money in the end, but the total number of debts might not move for a long time. If you struggle to stay motivated in the face of slow results, the snowball approach will work better for you.

The most important thing is to take consistent and ongoing action over time so you can reach debt freedom. You can also get creative and use a bit of both methods, by tackling the smallest balance first and then switching to the higher interest rate card and making movements as you find yourself losing or gaining motivation. Do what works for you and what you will remain committed to. Remember to set "debt pay-off" dates of celebration for small wins along the way.

Money Move

Getting out of bad debt will be a critical component of your financial plan and ultimately your success in building wealth.

Take time now to get organized and create a debt repayment plan:

- ☐ Make a list of all of your debt accounts, including balances owed, interest rates and minimum payments. Do some digging here to make sure you know the interest rates. This is usually the "shock factor" when you realize how much your debt is costing you.

- ☐ Once you have all credit card debt, personal loans, auto and student loans and mortgage(s) listed out, sort the accounts by interest rate highest to lowest and then again by balance, smallest to highest.

- ☐ Analyze credit card statements to determine what your debts will really "cost" if only making minimum payments each month, as the interest accumulates over time. For other loans, check out the amortization calculator at Bankrate.com to determine how much interest you'll pay over the life of the loan.

- ☐ Determine if you'll pay down debts using the snowball method to knock out balances quickly or the avalanche method to knock out the balances that are costing you the most first.

- ☐ Review your spending plan and identify areas where you can cut back in order to make progress towards your debt pay-off plan. Aim to put at least an extra few hundred dollars towards your debt each month. Target one balance to start; with and once paid off, roll all freed-up funds into the next balance.

Chapter 5:

SCHEDULE YOUR FINANCIAL CHECK-UP

"Know what you own, and know why you own it." ~ Peter Lynch

I'm a fan of going to the doctor. If there's something wrong with me physically, chances are they're the ones who are going to tell me how to fix it. When faced with the option of going in and talking to a real-life person or hitting up WebMD and fretting over all the things that "could" be wrong with me, I'll take the real-life consult any day. My husband, though? He'll drag out a cough for weeks and insist it's nothing, all the while letting the issue (and germs) spread throughout the household. I say this because he's doing it *right now*. He's not a fan of the doctor or feeling well, apparently.

When it comes to making sure your health checks out okay, are you the type that goes in every year for an annual physical or someone that skips out on the checkups until you've got a 103-degree fever, sweaty palms, and a super attractive phlegmy cough that sends people ducking for cover? The general recommendation is to make a visit at least annually to get your bill of clean health. Beyond your yearly checkup, scheduling appointments when an illness, injury or symptom pops up is key so you can get the recommended prescription or course of action to correct the issue and get things back to normal.

The same methodology applies to your finances. Whether you're the procrastinating kind or not, occasional checkups and reviews are necessary in order to ensure your money is staying the course to make your goals a reality. Where do you begin? When you're checking in on your financial health, there are five key questions to ask yourself:

IS YOUR NET WORTH GROWING?

Your net worth is your total financial worth, measured in dollars. Your net worth represents all of your assets (what you own) minus any financial liabilities or debt. It's important because maintaining a positive net worth (meaning owning *more* than you owe) not only keeps you on a positive financial course, but it can help you qualify for loans and more attractive credit terms, which goes back to saving you a lot of money over the long run. An important step on your path to workable wealth is to calculate your net worth. The initial calculation gives you a starting point to look back on over the coming months and years to make sure you're moving in the right direction, which is up, of course.

When crunching numbers for your net worth, take the following steps:

Tally up what you own. Begin by adding up the current market value of your assets, including your home, cash, savings accounts, stocks or mutual funds, retirement savings, valuable possessions such as jewelry or collectibles, and vehicles. If you need assistance determining the value of your home, Zillow can provide you with an estimate. If you need an estimate on what your car is worth, Kelley Blue Book can help.

Tally up what you owe. Next, itemize all of your financial liabilities, or money that you owe. This includes mortgage balances, auto loans, credit cards, student loans, and any other outstanding debt. You should have a list of the balances from the debt pay-down money moves in Chapter 4.

Subtract the total of what you owe from the total of what you own. This is your net worth. (You can see sample Net Worth Statements at the end of this chapter).

Track Your Financial Progress

It's time to treat your net worth just like your physical health, and hopefully you're ready to get in shape. If your doctor announced they need to run some tests because of an "abnormal" exam, you'd likely insist on finding out as many details about the problem as possible to determine a way to fix it. The same actions and perseverance should apply with your finances. If your net worth is in the red, meaning you owe more than you own, evaluate the details so you can understand how to address the issue now.

Your net worth is a benchmark for gauging whether or not your assets are increasing over time. If you're moving in a positive direction, bravo! However, you still need to ensure that you're continuously setting and achieving goals for ongoing growth. If your net worth is only holding steady or declining, you'll want to identify the causes and take action. Is your spending out of control? Are your investments not allocated properly? Are you not saving like you should be? To streamline the net worth tracking process for yourself, set up an Excel spreadsheet or use a website such as Mint to link up your accounts.

Repeating this exercise every six to twelve months allows you to compare current results with previous calculations so you can measure your progress.

HOW ARE YOUR FINANCIAL RATIOS?

Ratios and percentages can play a big part in making or breaking your financial future. These numbers provide more ways of analyzing your financial situation so you can know with confidence where you're at compared to where you want to be. In addition, regardless of goals, these numbers give you a better sense of the big picture when it comes to finances.

Debt-to-Income Ratio

Your debt-to-income (DTI) ratio is the percentage of your monthly income before taxes that must go towards paying off existing debt. The lower this ratio, the better. Lenders usually look at this number to determine what kind of a housing payment you can afford when it comes to obtaining a mortgage. Thirty-six percent is generally the maximum recommended DTI (which includes your mortgage), but I'd recommend aiming to keep your number below 33%.

When it comes to housing expenses, a good rule of thumb to consider is that no more than 28% of your gross monthly income should be used to pay for principal, interest, taxes and insurance.

Emergency Fund

Your emergency fund can protect you from the unexpected, and it's critical to have one in place. Ideally, you should aim to save three to six months' worth of "must have" expenses. If times get tough, you will hopefully cut back on your discretionary expenses immediately. If you have dependents, or have irregular income, you'll want to save a little more in your emergency fund.

Keep this cash in a liquid account so it's easily accessible when you need it. Remember, you don't have to achieve your goal of a fully funded emergency fund in a short period of time. It's more important to simply start saving for emergencies, even if it's just $10, $50, or $100 at a time. Set a goal of getting your first $1,000 stashed away and increase your savings from there.

Savings

If you're in your 20s and you're hoping for retirement in your 60s, aim to set aside at least 10% of your gross, pre-tax income. With 30-40 years on your side, starting with 10% now will really help you to take advantage of compounding interest. If you're in your 30s, you won't have as much time to stash away cash but you still have a decent period in front of you. Aim to save at least 15% of your gross income in order to make up for lost time.

ARE YOU SPENDING MORE THAN YOU EARN?

We've discussed this topic multiple times already. You know by now that if this is happening, your financial life needs a healthy dose of organization. Here's a quick recap of what you need to do to answer this question (and what needs to be adjusted if your answer is, "Yes, I'm spending too much."):

- Track your earnings and expenses.
- Set up a budget that works for you.
- If your spending exceeds your income, ask why.
- Address the behaviors or mindsets that underlie your overspending.
- Consider eliminating discretionary expenses or money you spend on "wants."
- Look into ways to reduce living expenses and fixed costs.

WHAT CHANGED IN THE PAST YEAR?

When we create plans for ourselves, they're often based upon where we are in our lives today. They account for current incomes, family sizes, careers, living situations, and so on. The issue is that life is fluid and ever changing. I always joke that plans become outdated the minute I complete them because bank accounts are fluctuating and some new life occurrence is happening.

When you're evaluating your financial health, it's important to review what's changed in the time since your last checkup. Did you get married, change jobs, move, make a big purchase, have a baby, start a business, receive an inheritance or get divorced? All of these are changes that could affect your goals, priorities and spending and savings patterns. Ensure you take time to adjust course to keep your finances on track.

DO YOUR INVESTMENTS NEED ADJUSTMENTS?

The stock market is a volatile place. While it's important to allocate your investments so they're in line with your goals, time horizon and risk tolerance, it's also important to remember to check in on your assets every six months in case there's need for change. We'll be digging into investments more in Chapter 6.

BOUNCING BACK FROM FINANCIAL MISTAKES

When you take the time to check in on your financial health, you're bound to come across an issue or two that's been swept under the rug. I've seen financial infidelity, maxed-out credit cards, forgotten loans, loans to family gone wrong, loans *from* family not paid back, shopping addictions, habit spending, and plain, old, genuine disinterest in gaining a financial education. So how do you bounce back from these money blunders and shake them off?

Acknowledge the Problem

The first step to solving any problem is admitting you have one. This is hard to do with money. Really hard. When you're used to burying your head in the sand or not paying attention to your finances enough to know what's going on (which is a problem in itself), it's difficult to realize something is actually out of place and a mistake has been or is being made.

It's time to call out the issue at hand and label it for what it is. Is it a loan from a family member or a friend that you haven't repaid? Do you have a shopping addiction? Maxed out credit cards? Is your rainy-day fund lacking or your credit score hitting new lows? Is it all of these things? Write it down, acknowledge it, and choose to take action to amend the issue.

Answer Some Questions

If you're in an unfortunate financial situation, this is not the time to point fingers or play the blame game. We're not here for the business of making excuses; we're here for the business of putting your money to work for you. Now is the time to reflect and dig into those fuzzy feelings you have about this money issue:

- How does being in this situation make you feel?

- What steps did you take that led you here?

- What beliefs do you have about money and the role it plays in your life? (Do you deserve to have savings, earn your salary or higher, be financially stable, or take an active role in your money? If the answer to any of these questions is no, it's likely a sign that this is an issue for you to explore deeper.)

- What habits have you formed that may need to be broken?

- What could you have done to prevent this and what are you willing to do to prevent it in the future?

- How will you hold yourself accountable?

Clean the Slate

In my early 20s I loaned a friend $1,000. I was helping her to get by on her bills and also still be able to hit the town when we wanted to blow off steam on the weekends. As time went on my loan went unpaid and the awkwardness grew exponentially. She never seemed to have the money to pay me back, and I ended up resentful. I learned a lot of lessons during that time, but the biggest was about communication and expectations. I likely wasn't clear enough in setting standards around the loan, and she felt uncomfortable discussing it altogether. Our friendship ended soon after and it was unfortunate.

If you owe somebody an explanation or some parameters and guidance, reach out. Inform your friends, family, utility company, bank, or whomever you need to about the issue you're facing, and let them know you're ready to work towards a solution. Be open and honest with them, and you'll likely receive a much better response than if you ignored the problem. If you've found that the problem is simply *you* and you're standing in your own way, then it's also time to come to terms there and set the wheels in motion for a fresh start.

Start Walking the Walk

Whether it's setting up a debt pay-down schedule, creating a monthly savings goal and automating contributions, writing letters to or calling creditors, or even setting up accountability check-ins with a friend or family member, do what needs to be done to get yourself back on track and rid yourself of the anxiety and guilt around money.

Keeping tabs on your financial health is essential in meeting your goals, and taking the time to figure out your net worth is similar to doing a personal inventory. You'll have all the facts, good and bad, right there in front of you and will be able to target the areas that are most important for improvement.

Money Move

Maintaining positive financial health can do more than fill your time with activities you enjoy and your home with items you love. Knowing you're on solid financial footing will also translate into less stress and more peace of mind, which translates into maintaining good physical health as well.

Take time now to evaluate your financial health.

☐ Gather bank and investment account statements, the value of your home, car and any collectibles, as well as credit card, mortgage and student loan statements.

☐ Calculate your net worth, following the formats on the next few pages. Determine if you're in the red or in the black.

☐ Review your financial ratios to determine where you stand. Specifically look at your emergency fund, savings rate and debt-to-income ratio. Go back to your cash flow (again) and make adjustments for each.

☐ Set a reminder on your calendar to check in on your net worth every six months.

SAMPLE ONE: CARLA'S NET WORTH

Assets

Cash

Synchrony Bank: Emergency Savings	$20,000	
Ally: Checking	$2,500	
Ally: Travel Savings	$4,000	
Ally: House Down Payment	$10,000	
		$36,500

Personal Accounts

Vanguard Account	$5,000	
		$5,000

Retirement Accounts

Vanguard: 401(k)	$65,500	
Vanguard: Rollover IRA	$18,000	
Vanguard: Roth IRA	$6,000	
		$89,500

Real Estate

N/A		$-

TOTAL ASSETS	$131,000

Liabilities

Real Estate

N/A	$-

Personal

Chase Credit Card (19%)	$(1,800)	
Amazon Credit Card (16%)	$(2,500)	
Nissan Auto (1.79%)	$(8,000)	
Student Loan (5.62%)	$(18,000)	
		$(30,300)

TOTAL LIABILITIES	$(30,300)

NET WORTH   **$100,700**

SAMPLE TWO: TIM AND SARAH'S NET WORTH

Assets

Cash

Chase Bank: Emergency Savings	$10,000	
Chase: Checking	$2,500	
Chase: Savings	$3,000	
		$15,500

Retirement Accounts

Tim: Fidelity 401(k)	$15,000	
Tim: Scottrade Roth IRA	$13,000	
Sarah: Vanguard 401 (k)	$26,000	
Sarah: Scottrade Roth IRA	$14,000	
		$68,000

Real Estate

Home: San Diego, CA	$550,000

TOTAL ASSETS	$633,500

Liabilities

Real Estate

Mortgage: San Diego, CA (30 yrs, 4%)	$(495,000)

Personal

Visa Credit Card (15%)	$(500)	
Ford Car Loan (0%)	$(15,000)	
		$(15,500)

TOTAL LIABILITIES	$(510,500)

NET WORTH	**$123,000**

Chapter 6:

INVEST FOR THE FUTURE

"Price is what you pay; value is what you get. Whether we're talking about socks or stocks, I like buying quality merchandise when it is marked down." ~ Warren Buffett

*C*heck with any media outlet in the past few years and they'll tell you Millennials and Gen Xers are afraid of the market. You'll read that we're sitting on piles of cash because we don't want to risk losing it. The media likes to underscore the fear and anxiety we supposedly hold about the stock market by listing a range of reasons as to the "likely" causes of our larger cash holdings or focus on saving instead of investing.

Nothing annoys me more than seeing these survey results proclaiming how terrified we are to invest our money, throwing out statistics of how many people have all of their money in cash as their proof. Why am I annoyed? Because based on my 12 years in the industry and the clients I work with, it's no secret to me that the investment world can be a confusing place. With fancy lingo, bears and bulls, percentages and a whole lot of ups and downs, I know that my clients aren't coming to me because they're *afraid* of the market. They, just like you, don't know where to actually put their money.

As I've stated before, there's a total disconnect between the financial planning industry and our generation, which unfortunately translates into a lack of an *investment education* for many. What's missing is an easy-to-follow, clear-cut plan of what to do with your money, where to put it, and how to start growing it. Investments don't have to be confusing. Saving for your future shouldn't be rocket science. It can be simple, fun, and easy to implement with just a bit of basic knowledge and plain-vanilla explanations. So let's toss the fancy industry lingo and get real. This is what you need to understand:

WAITING IS AN EXPENSIVE GAME

While waiting makes sense when it comes to impulse purchases and big-pocket-spending, it does *not* make sense when it comes to investing for your future. As much as we're concerned with treating ourselves today, looking out for our future selves is just as (if not more) important.

The more you push your future self into "tomorrow" land, the more you'll be hurting when it comes time to play the catch-up game. Thinking you have plenty of time to worry about retirement can be a costly mistake. Yes, it can feel like there simply isn't enough to go around when there's rent or mortgages to pay, student loans to manage and families to raise. I totally understand that you have expenses, bills and other financial goals and priorities to meet. However, before you justify your willingness to wait with retirement being *decades* into your future, you might want to think again to fully understand the cost of waiting.

YOUR MONEY'S BEST FRIEND

Meet your money's best friend, *compound interest*. When you invest, you earn interest on your money. You then earn interest on that interest. This is called *compound interest*. It's this extra bit of compounding and growing that can really make a difference over the course of a working career. Let's see how it works and the benefits by looking at Eleanor and Lauren, two friends who started saving at different times, as an example below:

Case #1: Imagine our friend Early Eleanor starts saving for retirement at age 25. Even though she has student loans and a car payment, she consciously invests $100 a month for 10 years and stops at the age of 35. By the age of 35, she's contributed $12,000 and with interest of 6%, her balance will have grown to $15,996.04.

She leaves these savings in a retirement account and doesn't touch the account until the age of 65. Assuming the annual return rate continues at 6%, she'll have $91,873.11 when she turns 65.

Case #2: If Early Eleanor contributed $100 for 20 years instead of 10, she would have contributed $24,000. With interest, she will have $44,463.42 in her account. After leaving the account alone until 65, at retirement she will have $142,600.21.

Case #3: Unfortunately, our friend Late Lauren didn't make retirement contributions at the age of 25. She couldn't get her spending under control and was too focused on living for today. Instead, Lauren waited until age 35 to start investing and contributed $100 a month for 10 years until age 45. She received the same return of 6%.

Even though she contributed and earned the same amounts, her account will be worth only $51,301.47 at age 65. That's already a close to $40,000 difference from Early Eleanor *just* because she waited to start!

Case #4: Even if Late Lauren contributes $100 for 20 years, her account will only be worth $79,627.21 when she wants to retire at 65 – much less than Early Eleanor.

Case	Saver	Age	No. of Years Contributing $100/Month	Total Amount Saved (with interest)
1	Early Eleanor	25-35	10	$15,996.04
2	Early Eleanor	25-45	20	$44,463.42
3	Late Lauren	35-45	10	$15,996.04
4	Late Lauren	35-55	20	$44,463.42

Case	Years to Compound (no Additional Contributions)	Balance at 65	Money Earned From Interest
1	30	$91,873.11	$79,873.11
2	20	$142,600.21	$118,600.21
3	20	$51,301.47	$39,301.47
4	10	$79,627.21	$55,627.21

When looking at Late Lauren, who saved for 20 years compared to Early Eleanor, who saved for 10 years, you'll see that Lauren was unable to match Eleanor's savings. Eleanor has $40,572 more than Lauren in the 10-year period, and $62,973 more than her in the 20-year period!

That's a pretty significant difference that occurred simply because Early Eleanor, in both cases, gave her savings more time to compound and grow. Saving early makes a big difference. Waiting is expensive!

HOW MUCH DO I NEED TO INVEST?

I can't tell you how many times I've been asked, "How much should I have saved by now?" or "How far behind am I for retirement?" You already know the importance of investing for your retirement and growing your wealth. But the question still remains: How much should you contribute to make sure you actually have enough built up when you need it? To be honest, it depends. The exact number you need may be a bit difficult to pinpoint, but there are some ways to plan based on your goals and a few general rules of thumb you can use to ballpark how much you need to invest.

Think About Your Unique Goals and Needs

Imagine you're shopping with a friend. You're both searching for a new pair of jeans. Chances are that the pair that looks best on you will be a different size, look and feel than the pair that works best for your friend. Even though the idea of matching outfits could be a great Instagram opportunity, you likely won't find the same solution for the both of you.

This also goes for your investments and savings. Ultimately, there's not a one-size-fits-all answer to the question of how much everyone should save. How much *you* should save depends on your goals, what you'd like to accomplish in life, and how you want your future to look.

If you're reading this chapter, you've hopefully already established what type of short- and long-term goals interest you. Think about when you hope to retire. It is at 60? 50? Tomorrow? Would you want to cut off work completely or transition to part time for a few years first? Or do you love what you're doing so much that you can't imagine ever stopping? Whether you want to hustle now to enjoy later, or enjoy now *and* later, or just enjoy today and keep at it until you can't any longer, will effect how much you need to stash away. Keep in mind that even if you plan to work until the end, you *may* have to stop working at some point due to age and health issues, which is why it's important to plan ahead. Ask yourself what your retirement lifestyle looks like and how much it will cost you per year to maintain.

If you want to spend most of your time traveling, a year in retirement will cost you more than if you wanted to spend most of your time enjoying your home, having family and friends over, and volunteering for your favorite cause. Neither one of these situations is "better" than the other, but financially speaking, they look *really* different.

Envision your ideal lifestyle after work (and when you'll need to start drawing from your investments). Then take some educated guesses on your costs and expenses and create a mock yearly budget for yourself. Multiplying that budget over a period of years (like 25, 30 or 40) will give you an idea of the total amount you'll need in your nest egg before you can retire. You can work backward from there to determine how much you need to invest each month during your working career to meet that goal.

Two Rules of Thumb

While there's no one right answer, trying to figure things out down to the last cent in your situation can be overwhelming and way too complicated. Get yourself into a realistic ballpark by starting with these common rules of thumb:

The 4% Rule: The 4% Rule helps show you how much you can withdraw annually in retirement. Let's say you retire with $800,000 in your portfolio. The 4% rule says that, in order to stay solvent throughout your retirement years, you should withdraw no more than 4% of that $800,000 – or $32,000 a year. Determine how much you need to live on and back into what you need to have invested to make that 4% equal to your annual expenses.

Invest in Percentages: Because many of these numbers in investments and retirement revolve around the income you earn, it makes sense to target percentages to save in lieu of hard numbers. If you're in your 20s, aim to save 10% to 15% of your gross income, increasing to 15% to 20% in your 30s. With your income constantly growing, make note that every time you receive a raise, you should increase your savings percentage by at least 1% to 2%. Oftentimes a raise contributes to lifestyle inflation and more money being spent, rather than looking at it as an opportunity to increase savings.

Keep in mind your investment strategy may be fluid as you're likely working towards multiple goals at once. For example, if you're looking to buy a home in a few years, that will alter the amount you're putting towards retirement savings. Or if you're tackling debt, perhaps you save what you can now and then go full force once you're debt-free. The important thing is to just get started. Every little bit counts.

ALL YOUR EGGS + ONE BASKET = HIGH RISK OF SCRAMBLED EGGS

How many times have you been told, "Don't put all your eggs in one basket"? Drop the basket and you risk smashing all your eggs, which leaves you with nothing. If you divide the eggs into a few baskets, however, you'll still have some left for breakfast if you accidentally drop one of those baskets.

As an investor, it's important to make sure you don't put your nest egg into one basket. What if you invested all of your money in Starbucks stock (because you truly, 100% believe it's the world's best coffee), and then Peet's Coffee, Dunkin Donuts, Caribou Coffee or others perform better? What will happen to your money? (Hint: you'll probably lose some.)

If a competing brand is taking over market share, it may not bode well for your investment. Or what if a world report comes out claiming coffee is terrible for your health? (Hopefully that never happens. I consider coffee one of my dearest friends.) However, with all of your money invested *in* coffee, what do you think would happen to the value of your accounts? This is why it's important to diversify.

WHAT IS DIVERSIFICATION?

Look in your closet. Chances are you own more than just one pair of shoes, right? You've got dress shoes, tennis shoes, workout shoes, sandals, boot, slippers, and more. Now imagine you only had one pair of those shoes to wear every day, no matter what your wardrobe consists of or what your responsibilities are for the day. You'd look pretty silly heading into a winter storm in your sandals, to the beach in your snow boots or wearing your slippers with your suit to work. (Unless you work from home, in which case slippers all day are totally acceptable.) You've had to diversify your shoes to best align with activities, outfits, and the variety of hats you wear. Having only one pair would be risky to your health (and your fashion sense).

Diversification is a key element to a successful investment strategy and even if you're sitting on hundreds of thousands of dollars, it could be a tough thing to achieve by just picking out random stocks. Diversification is the strategy of spreading out your investments to reduce risk and smooth out the ups and downs of the market. To diversify properly, you'll want to diversify *between* asset categories and *within* asset categories. (Think different types of shoes and the number you have of each type. How many different types or pairs of sandals or boots do you own?)

The basic asset classes are stocks, bonds and cash. Each class will have greater returns under different economic circumstances. Historically, stocks have a higher return over long time horizons, but are more volatile. If you're investing for a short-term goal, it's possible your stock might be worth less than the buying price when you want to sell, which should make you hesitant about putting things like your emergency fund or home down payment money into the market. Bonds provide regular income and vary less than stocks but historically have a lower return. Cash accounts are the safest of all but also return the least over time. If you've checked the interest rate on your savings account lately, chances are you already know your money isn't exactly hard at work for you.

Stocks allow you to own a piece of a company, while bonds enable you to loan a company money while it pays you an interest rate in return for your loan. But who actually has time to look into each and every company to make sure it's a solid investment before dropping your cash in? And how many people actually enjoy digging that far into the numbers? Not to mention the number of spreadsheets it will take.

With little time on your side and a lack of investment credentials, mutual funds and exchange-traded funds (ETFs) are an excellent way to streamline your diversification. These funds pool together money from a group of investors and purchase stocks, bonds and other securities. The fund acts as one investment. As the underlying securities increase or decrease in value, so does the overall value of the fund. Each fund has a strategy and overall objective. Some may be geared towards growth and others may be geared towards income generation or stability. When you buy a mutual fund or ETF, you buy a collection of many stocks or bonds at once, allowing you to have a diverse asset allocation even with an investment of just $1,000.

COMMON INVESTING QUESTIONS (AND MY ANSWERS)

When it comes to investing, it's hard to know where to begin. Here are five questions I'm faced with on an ongoing basis from readers and clients:

Where should I invest my emergency fund? Your emergency fund is meant for emergencies, and last I checked, we don't actually know when those are going to happen. Due to the lack of timeliness of these events, it doesn't make sense to invest this money into the stock market and risk having to sell or pull out at an inopportune time. Open a separate savings account to hold these funds and consider holding these cash reserves in an online high-yield savings account at Synchrony Bank, which currently pays up to 1.05% or Ally Bank, which currently pay up to 1%.

How do I get started with investing? If you're just getting started in the investment world, you'll want to begin with a retirement account. If you have access to a 401(k) or retirement plan through your employer, start there. Otherwise, consider opening a Traditional or Roth IRA on your own with a company like Vanguard. These accounts are covered in the section below.

What are the hot stocks today? If you're looking to make your money with a hot stock, you're better off taking your cash to Vegas. Just don't do it. However, if you insist on playing in the market, I recommend only doing so after you've contributed to retirement and allocating just 5% of your portfolio to stocks and funds you'd like to explore.

How do I know I'm picking the right investments for retirement? When saving for your retirement, whether within your employer's provided retirement plan or on your own, chances are you've seen a target date fund as an investment option. These types of mutual funds make diversification much easier with an asset allocation that is set according to a selected time frame (for example, your target retirement year). The allocation starts off more aggressive and becomes more conservative as the "target date" approaches and you need access to the money. Target date funds are a great and easy way to allocate your money, but it's still important to research the fund's underlying allocation, expense ratio and returns before jumping in. You can typically find all of this information directly on the fund company's website or in the fund prospectus.

What if I've already maxed out my retirement savings? If you're already contributing the maximum allowable to your retirement savings, it's time to open an after-tax brokerage account and begin stashing away your money there. It's important to note the timeline of when you'll want access to these funds before investing. If they're still meant for retirement, stocks can play a bigger role. If you're looking to use this money in the next few years, however, you'll want to stick to a much more conservative route (think cash and CD's) to ensure you don't lose principal.

MAKE SMART CHOICES FOR YOUR RETIREMENT

Your chances of winning the lottery are 1 in 175 million. The status of Social Security when you retire is questionable altogether. If you want to head into your retirement years with financial peace of mind, then you're going to have to forge the path yourself. Your best place to start is with one or more of the below retirement accounts.

Traditional Individual Retirement Account (IRA): An IRA allows you to contribute pretax income (up to a certain threshold) to an investment account. This money grows tax deferred, meaning you pay no taxes on principal (i.e. your contributions) and earnings until funds are withdrawn from the account. For 2016, tax-deductible contributions may be made up to $5,500 to an IRA account. Penalty-free withdrawals from your IRA can begin at age 59 1/2 and become mandatory at age 70 1/2. Translation: You're saving money on your taxes at today's rates, but you'll be paying a future (possibly higher) rate upon withdrawal.

Roth Individual Retirement Account (Roth IRA): A Roth IRA is similar to the above Traditional IRA except that contributions are made with *after-tax* income and, therefore, are not tax deductible. For 2016, non-tax-deductible contributions may be made up to $5,500. Contribution limits phase out above certain income thresholds, meaning if you earn above a certain limit, you may not qualify to make Roth IRA contributions. There is no mandatory age for withdrawal and there are no taxes due on principal or earnings upon withdrawal from the Roth IRA after age 59 ½ (and for a few other unique situations). Translation: You're paying taxes up front at today's rate, instead of paying the (possibly higher) rates in place when you begin withdrawals.

401(k): 401(k) plans are retirement accounts sometimes offered through an employer. The 401(k) can come with a Traditional or a Roth option depending on your employer offerings. For 2016, tax-deductible (for a Traditional) or after-tax (for a Roth) contributions can be made up to $18,000. Contributions are deducted automatically from your paycheck. For the Traditional option, funds will grow tax deferred until withdrawal. For the Roth option, there will be no taxes on principal or earnings at withdrawal. Note: If you receive an employer match on your 401(k) contributions, you are still allowed to personally contribute up to $18,000. Anything kicked in from your employer is extra icing on the cake.

403(b): A 403(b) is similar to a 401(k) except this account applies to employees of public education organizations and some nonprofits.

Solo 401(k): A Solo 401(k) is a traditional 401(k) that covers a business owner with no employees or that person and his or her spouse. A business owner can make elective deferrals up to 100% of earned income up to an annual maximum contribution of $18,000 in 2016, and employer non-elective contributions of 25% of compensation, with total contributions not to exceed $53,000 for 2016.

Simplified Employee Pension (SEP) IRA: A SEP IRA is a retirement account for entrepreneurs that allows for a contribution up to 25% of each employee's pay (and 25% of your net self-employment income). Annual contributions are limited to the smaller of $53,000 or 25% of compensation for 2016.

Savings Incentive Match Plan for Employees (SIMPLE) IRA: A SIMPLE IRA is a retirement plan designed for and available to any small business with 100 or fewer employees. The employer is required to contribute each year either a matching contribution of 3% of compensation, or 2% non-elective contribution for each eligible employee (meaning the employer contributes even if the employee doesn't). An employee can contribute $12,500 in 2016.

THE MOST IMPORTANT THING ABOUT INVESTING: JUST DO IT

You now know that compound interest is your money's best friend. The longer you wait to start investing for your future, the more distance there will be between these two (and the more making up you'll have to do in the long run). Get started with investing by leveraging your employer-sponsored retirement plan or by opening a retirement account of your own. Look to mutual funds and ETFs as a way to efficiently and effectively diversify your money, and don't forget that some accounts are meant to be held in cash.

If you have an employer match on retirement account contributions, take advantage of the free money offered first and then review your tax and income situation to make the decision on where the rest of your retirement savings should go. If you're like many investors, your retirement funds will likely consist of a mix-and-match with a few different account types, so don't feel like you need to stick with just one account. If you've maxed out your 401(k) and Roth IRA for the year, move over to saving in a personal, after-tax account to build up your nest egg even more.

Slow and steady will win the race on this one, so keep a level head, set up systematic monthly contributions, understand your ability to handle market swings, and leverage the help of a CFP® professional if you feel uncomfortable handling things solo. You'll then find your way to a healthy retirement without the stress and anxiety that many people have around their finances.

Money Move

You work hard for your money. Now it's time to put it to work for you. Retirement is inevitable, and investing your money appropriately will help to get you there on solid ground.

Take time to complete these Money Moves:

- ☐ Evaluate the retirement plan options available to you through your employer or to you individually and select which account(s) you'll move forward with.

- ☐ Open any necessary accounts. Vanguard, Scottrade and E*TRADE are great custodians to start with if you need to open your own account.

- ☐ Calculate a ballpark figure of how much you need to save for retirement using a rule of thumb – either the percentage rule or the 4% withdrawal rule.

- ☐ Begin systematic monthly contributions to your retirement account, aiming to increase whenever possible.

- ☐ Select an investment allocation based upon your risk tolerance and time frame for goals.

- ☐ Schedule time to review retirement plans and investments every six months for adjustments and increases in your contributions.

Chapter 7:

PROTECT YOUR A$$ETS

"Time is more valuable than money. You can get more money, but you cannot get more time." ~ Jim Rohn

'm the first to admit that I'm a catastrophizer. I could kick your butt in a "what-if" battle any day. *"What if you lose your job?" "What if they get into a car accident?" "What if cancer comes into play?"* Part of this mentality is because I'm paid to think this way. The other part is that I'm generally concerned for the well-being of my loved ones, friends, clients and readers (that means you).

No one likes to talk about the bad things that happen in life. Dying, injuries and illnesses – it's uncomfortable. Try having the "Would you want me to get remarried if something happened to you?" conversation with your spouse. If that doesn't put a lump in your throat, I don't know what will. It's easy to sweep these conversations and the questions that come with them under the rug, but inevitably, you *will* face them. As Benjamin Franklin said, "In this world, nothing can be certain except death and taxes."

"IT WON'T HAPPEN TO ME"

As much as we like to think we're invincible, we're not. In my business and personal life alone, I've seen people in their 20s, 30s and 40s diagnosed with cancer, widowed, out of work due to an accident, in the hospital for months due to high-risk pregnancies, deemed uninsurable due to past medical histories, and more. Our generation faces scare upon scare with lumps and bumps that pop up over time.

It's easy to think, "It won't happen to me," but the stark reality is it could and it might. Sickness, injury and disaster don't just happen to others. They happen to people like you and me on a daily basis and at any given time. This is why it's so important to think about these "what-ifs" today and create a plan so in the event something does occur, your wishes are documented, your income is protected, and the right decision-makers are put in place.

YOUR MOST VALUABLE ASSET YOU'RE LIKELY FORGETTING

Take inventory of all of your possessions and the balances of your checking and savings accounts. Which would you say is the most valuable to you? Is it the bank account with the highest value? The piece of jewelry that's been in the family for years? Your laptop or flat screen TV? Your most valuable asset probably isn't in a bank or a tangible thing. Your most valuable asset is the one that is currently bringing in all of your money. And that's your ability to earn an income. Think about how much you make each year and multiply that by the period you have until retirement. Don't forget to include raises, bonuses and promotions. How much money do you think that would add up to?

Your income comes from your talents, skills, education, and your ability to actually *do the job*. So what would you say if I told you that you have a 25% chance of becoming disabled before you retire? According to the Social Security Administration, that's exactly what could happen. Over one in four of today's 20-year-olds will experience some form of disability before age 67.[6]

What happens if you can't actually perform your work? What would that do to your lifestyle, your family and your goals? What happens if you're no longer able to actually earn your income? This is where disability insurance comes into play.

As Americans, we insure our cars, our cell phones, our pets and more – but for most, insuring your income is set aside or just plain ignored. People think, "It won't happen to me," or perceive disability as something that happens only to the elderly. In reality, long-term disabilities can manifest in the form of pregnancy complications, cancers, mental disorders, injuries, poisonings, and more.[7] According to the Council for Disability Awareness, the average long-term disability claim lasts 34.6 months.[8] That's almost three years, meaning your average emergency fund likely won't protect you for the full term.

WHAT IS DISABILITY INSURANCE?

Disability insurance is a plan that provides for periodic payments of benefits when a disabled insured is unable to work. The insurance is designed to replace anywhere from 45% to 66 2/3% of your gross income should illness or injury keep you from earning an income in your occupation. It encompasses paid sick leave, short-term disability benefits (STD), and long-term disability benefits (LTD).

Short-Term Disability (STD)

Short-term disability coverage kicks in if you're out of work for a brief period, typically ranging from a few weeks up to 90 days. Elimination periods are usually about a week or so before the benefits be-

---

[6] http://www.ssa.gov/dibplan/index.htm
[7] http://www.disabilitycanhappen.org/research/CDA_LTD_Claims_Survey_2014.asp
[8] http://www.disabilitycanhappen.org/chances_disability/

gin (income can be supplemented with sick or vacation time during this period). The policy pays up to 66 and 2/3% of your income until the benefits run out or your long-term policy kicks in. So if you're making $1,500 a week, the policy may pay you up to $1,000.

Long-Term Disability (LTD)

Long-term disability policies pay up to 66 and 2/3% of your income for an extended period of time. This is typically until you return to work, max out the policy for a certain number of years, or reach retirement age. Elimination periods usually range around a few months but can be longer, and benefits kick in after your short-term benefits run out (if you have such a policy).

CONSIDERATIONS FOR DISASTER-PROOFING YOUR INCOME

When obtaining or reviewing an income protection policy, look for and ask the following:

- Does your employer provide coverage? If so, is it for short or long term and what are the benefits and elimination periods?

- Whether a group policy or a privately owned policy, ensure you read the fine print and understand maximum benefits, terms and definitions.

- Is it "any" or "own" occupation coverage? (Does it pay if you can't perform your own occupation or *any* job that meets your education and skill level?)

- How much of your income will ultimately be replaced and for how long?

- What is the elimination period or how long until the policy kicks in?

- How much should you have stashed away to cushion any elimination periods? (Will you save and self-insure for any short-term disabilities?)

- Will the benefits be pre-tax or post-tax? (This comes into play when participating in employer group policies. If you're paying premiums pre-tax or the company pays for you, your benefits will be taxable.)

Keep in mind that you can't replace 100% of your income with disability insurance. The goal is to provide protection, but also to give you an incentive to return to work.

KNOW YOUR INSURANCE POLICY OPTIONS

Before you look into a private policy, check with your employer to determine if they provide you with access to a group policy. They may provide and pay for it as a part of your benefits *or* they may provide you with the option of purchasing it. Either way, this will likely be the most affordable route for you to receive coverage. Just ensure you know the parameters of the policy.

If you don't have access to disability insurance through your employer or you're an entrepreneur and need to obtain a private policy, ensure you're looking at your earnings over the two most recent years when applying for coverage. In addition, look at any associations for which you may qualify for membership within your industry and determine if they offer group disability insurance as a member benefit. This may be a more affordable route to access coverage when self-employed.

#YOLO: SO DON'T FORGET YOUR LIFE INSURANCE

Has there ever been a truer hashtag than #YOLO (you only live once)? This hashtag phenomenon has been the cause for some people taking amazing and brave actions in their lives. For others, it's an excuse to do some incredibly ridiculous stuff. Whichever side of the spectrum you fall on, the fact is that you *will* only live once. If that's the case, and we know it's inevitable that something will happen to each of us, why is life insurance an often ignored and under prioritized need in the majority of financial situations?

If you're married, have children, or have anyone in your life who depends on your income, how would your salary be replaced in the event of your death? Would your spouse be able to maintain the household expenses? What about the mortgage payment? Whether you're the main breadwinner, contributing a portion of the household income, or staying at home with the kids, you make valuable contributions. These might be financial, in the form of an income, or through the activities that you perform that would cost your family money to replace (like child care). Both types of value should be protected.

When it comes to what type of policy to purchase, a 20- or 30-year term policy will almost always be the most affordable and appropriate option for you. If there is someone trying to sell you any other type of life insurance policy aside from term insurance, ask them how much commission they'll be making off of the sale. Request that they detail exactly what you'll be paying in fees over time. That alone should point you back in the direction of term insurance.

Here's what to consider when evaluating the amount of life insurance you need:

Income Replacement and Timeframe

How much income would your family need if something were to suddenly happen to you and for what time period? For example, if you're 30, married, and have a child at home, you may need your life insurance to cover costs until your child is 18 and then until your spouse retired at age 65. This includes amounts they would need to maintain lifestyle and household expenses. Be sure to account for other income sources available such as your spouse's wages, interest and dividend payments, and so on.

Debt Load

Consider the outstanding balances on any mortgages, car loans, and any other types of debt. Total these values and incorporate the number into your life insurance face value. Being able to pay off these balances would decrease the income replacement percentage that your spouse or family would need if they lost your income.

College Expenses

If you're planning to pay for all or a portion of your children's college expenses, it's best to look up the average cost of college in today's dollars. According to Savingforcollege.com, the cost of a four-year degree at a public university for those with in-state residency is $39,000 in 2015 and will be $94,800 18 years from now not including room/board, books and other fees)![9] Start by incorporating today's costs into your policy and reevaluate over time. If something were to happen to you today, the proceeds could be invested and allocated in such a way to grow and keep up with future expenses.

Final Expenses

Depending on the type of service you want, final expenses can range from a few thousand to $15,000 or more. A general rule of thumb is to include $10,000 to $15,000 in the face value of your policy to cover final expenses.

Current Asset Level

Be sure to consider any amounts that you already have stocked away such as savings accounts and money markets, 401(k)s, IRAs, Roth IRAs, stocks and mutual funds. These are assets that will also grow over time and help to supplement income needs.

---

[9]   http://www.savingforcollege.com/tutorial101/the_real_cost_of_higher_education.php

The Value of What You Do

Even though one spouse may stay at home, there is still value provided through activities such as child care, housekeeping, yard work, and more that would have to be replaced by either the surviving spouse taking over these responsibilities or paying for someone else to provide a service. Be sure to incorporate these expenses into your life insurance needs estimate.

The most interesting part about life insurance is that it's *not* about you. It's about your family and making sure they're protected in case something happens to you.

Keep in mind that the amount of life insurance you and/or your spouse need will change over time as your situation changes. With family additions, home purchases and upgrades, income level fluctuations and more, the amount of your insurance coverage should be evaluated on an annual basis or immediately after a change to your financial situation at a minimum.

SHOP 'TIL YOU DROP

When it comes to both disability and life insurance, shop around to different carriers and don't settle on the first product or provider you see. You'll want to ensure you're getting the best policy for your money, and by looking at just one company, you're limiting the scope of options available to you.

By working with a broker instead of an agent, you'll have access to a bigger variety of companies. Ultimately, you'll want to talk to a CFP® before purchasing a policy of your own in order to ensure you're getting the right coverage and protection. Working with professionals can also help you avoid going down a rabbit hole of comparing too many companies, leaving you overwhelmed and unsure of which choice is best.

YOU CAN'T TAKE IT WITH YOU

You likely own things: Cars, clothes, electronics, bank accounts, jewelry. This is what makes up your estate; and believe it or not, you do have one. Your estate is what you own, and no matter how big or how little it is, you can't take it with you when you die, which means that you need to address what happens to those items today.

Chances are you're focused on living your best life now. Estate planning might seem like something to tackle when you're older (or richer). But if you have assets, and especially if you have anyone depending on you, you need to take care of this important financial planning task. An estate plan provides peace of mind that your loved ones are taken care of, even if the worst were to happen.

An estate plan is something that, upon your death, will guide the transfer of your assets according to your wishes, minimize the transaction costs of the transfer, provide liquid money for common costs, and protect and provide for loved ones.

If you don't have your affairs in order, state law will dictate the processing of your estate, and you might not like the result. Given the choice, wouldn't you rather your estate be handled by your family — not the courts — in the way you see fit?

When thinking about your need for an estate plan, consider the following:

- How do you want your personal assets to be distributed? Who stands to inherit them?

- Are there certain items or gifts that you would want to go to specific people? (For example, your assets could pass to your spouse, but you could indicate your grandmother's jewelry be passed to your sister or your DVD collection be donated to a local charity.)

There are a variety of documents that need to be put into place to best articulate and share your wishes with friends and family. The items below are the best to get started on:

Create a **Will**. This allows you to appoint an executor of your estate and provide details on how your assets should be distributed in the event of your death.

A **Durable Power of Attorney** appoints a representative, such as a spouse, sibling or parent, to perform certain actions on your behalf, such as paying bills and making financial decisions, if you're unable to perform these tasks yourself. Ask yourself, in case of a medical emergency, who do I want responsible for making decisions on my behalf if I'm unable to?

An **Advanced Healthcare Directive (or Living Will)** documents which types of medical care, including life-sustaining treatments, you deem to be appropriate or inappropriate should you become incapacitated, while a **Medical Power of Attorney** designates a representative to carry out those wishes, if needed.

If you have young children, who do you want to care for them should something happen to you and your spouse? **Guardianship provisions,** which can be stated in a Will or Trust, will document your wishes. Without appointing someone, any interested parties, ranging from family friends to relatives to social services agencies, may apply for guardianship through the courts.

IT'S NOT ABOUT YOU

I totally get that the above can be daunting to think about or even complete, which makes putting it on the back burner pretty easy. Keep in mind, though, that creating an estate plan is one of the most lasting gifts you will leave behind. Not only can it act as a form of insurance and risk management when used properly, but it *will* also make it easier for your family to move forward with healing and rebuilding.

No one likes to think about his or her own death or disability. That's why so many families are unprepared when the worst does happen.

The best time to start is now. Even if money is tight, you can keep the costs in line by starting with the basics. Your estate plan can evolve over time.

Taking the Next Step

Ready to create your estate plan to protect yourself, your possessions, and your loved ones? You might be considering using one of those legal sites online, but it's probably not worth the money. Estate planning is very complex, and it varies from state to state. A document created from a do-it-yourself website might not hold up in a court of law. You might as well save your money and put it towards the cost of an estate attorney.

Look for an estate attorney licensed in your area. Consider asking a financial advisor or a CPA for recommendations of good estate lawyers. Interview a few lawyers and you'll find the one that's right for you.

Once in place, your estate plan (including any beneficiary designations on retirement accounts or life insurance policies) should be reviewed annually to ensure documents and designations remain aligned with your current state of affairs and wishes.

Take the first step towards putting an estate plan in place today. It's not fun or easy, but it's a great help to your loved ones if the worst were to happen.

Money Move

Although we consider ourselves superheroes, we're not invincible. For your sake and for your family, it's time to get organized and protect your assets.

Take time to complete these Money Moves:

☐ If employed, review your company benefits and the options available to you for disability and life insurance. If you're not already enrolled, update your benefit elections to take advantage of this coverage.

☐ If your employer disability insurance covers less than 66 2/3% of your income, or if you're self-employed or don't have access to coverage, enlist the help of an insurance broker to evaluate options available for private insurance coverage.

☐ Calculate the amount of life insurance you need. (Personally, I like the Life Insurance Needs calculator available at Life Happens.) Factor in the amount of coverage provided by any employers, then reach out to an insurance broker to obtain a 20- or 30-year term insurance policy for the remainder. Note: If you don't anticipate staying at your employer for long, consider obtaining full insurance coverage through a private insurer.

☐ Have the tough conversations. Consider what you'd want to happen to your assets, your children, and whom you'd want to make decisions if something happened to you. Seek out estate planning attorney referrals in your area and work to create a personalized plan.

Chapter 8:

OPTIMIZE YOUR INCOME

"An investment in knowledge pays the best interest."
~ Benjamin Franklin

A couple of years ago, I was asked to write a letter to my younger self. This letter was included in a presentation that contained excerpts from several successful women in the business world, imparting their lessons learned on their journey to a successful career.

Aside from the fact that I was incredibly humbled to be included in such a presentation, the writing of my letter served as a source of reflection, gratitude, and a sheer confidence boost as to all that had transpired over the previous ten years. In a time when it seemed everyone was questioning what I was doing and the fear of taking two steps back instead of three steps forward was high, this is the letter I wrote to myself:

Mary Beth,

It may be hard to see the light right now. It's hard to be the youngest kid on the block and even harder to do so in a male-dominated industry. You feel insecure and out of place. Sometimes you even feel angry because you're being intentionally made to feel as if you're out of place.

I know you're questioning if you're on the right track. Wondering if you should switch career paths and get out of the personal finance business altogether. Trust me when I tell you to stick with it. Not for the money or because you don't want to let anyone down. Stick with it because this is your passion.

Your career may not be evolving the way you had hoped it would, but the experiences you're having and the opportunities (perceived or not) are shaping you into exactly who you need to be in order to reach your dreams. There will be hard days, and a lot of them at that. You'll work hard, be tested and struggle. You'll face ageism, sexism, and a lot of other isms on your climb up the career ladder.

Ultimately, you'll learn that nobody will look out for you like you will, how to take constructive criticism with grace, that the life-long learning model is the best model, and you'll build a support network of entrepreneurs, mentors and colleagues who will assist you in following your passion and building something bigger than you could have imagined.

Don't discount the tough times and difficult people in your career, because those are the lessons that will stick the most. Also, continue to advocate for yourself. Learn to compromise, but continue to seek the positions, income and opportunities that you believe you are worth. You have the drive and work ethic to get where you want to be; you just need to have the confidence in yourself and your skills to get there.

It will happen for you. It will be a windy, curvy road, as you've heard most career paths are, but you will launch your own business before the age of 30. It will be the scariest and most liberating experience of your life, but one that you can handle. Believe it or not, you will become one of those people that others will turn to for professional and career advice. You'll coach your peers, students and those older than you.

You'll surprise yourself, Mary Beth, in more ways than you can imagine. Keep at it and you'll touch more lives and effect change where you were told you couldn't.

Your Older Self

When I wrote that letter, it became very apparent just how much I had invested in myself throughout my career. How hard I had pushed, negotiated, hustled and sacrificed for career moves, strategic transitions and the ability to pursue a craft that I am 100% passionate about. It didn't happen overnight, and I wish my younger self was able to read this letter so I could have fully understood the importance of investing in myself.

I went to college for financial planning. I worked in the industry during college. I took all the courses necessary to sit for the CERTI-FIED FINANCIAL PLANNER™ designation while I was in school, allowing me to take the ridiculously hard two-day exam upon graduation. One of the owners of the firm I worked at during the time was also taking the classes necessary to sit for the CFP® exam.

Imagine my surprise when he told me one day that I "couldn't sit for the CFP® exam" until he could. It was an eye-opening experience and one of those life lessons that I've carried with me since. He was looking out for himself. He didn't want to look bad with a younger employee getting a designation before him. Although I felt I had worked hard for them, I realized that there was a ceiling at that firm that I wouldn't be able to pass. I left shortly after.

When it comes to growing your income and earning what you're worth, *nobody will look out for you like you look out for you.* I repeat: Nobody will look out for you like *you* look out for you. There is no one in your life under a direct obligation to tell you you're doing an amazing job and to pay you top dollar for your skills. *Should* your employers and clients do that? Yes. Do they *have* to? Absolutely not. If you want to earn more, it's on you to make that happen.

INVEST IN YOURSELF

Your human capital is your ability to earn (or command) an income. It includes your skill set, expertise, education, and ability to connect or interact with others. In financial terms, your human capital is the present value of all your future wages. It matters most for you because of the value it will continue to provide over the next 20 to 40 years by funding your lifestyle and allowing you to save for current and future goals.

As much as we'd like to stash away all of the money that comes in for us, much of it will go back out the door. Whether your cash goes towards bills, lifestyle needs and events today, or you put it into a holding account to be allocated towards a future goal, that money will be spent. This is why increasing your income is such an important step and investment on your road to workable wealth. Increasing your human capital gives you the ability to increase your net worth, which puts you in a better position to meet your goals.

Although you may have a degree or two under your belt, there's no reason to limit your potential to earn an income to those pieces of paper alone. You provide a value and a service to others no matter what you do. It's important to make the most of what you can offer. Here are some strategies to reflect on and items to consider when it comes to investing in your ability to earn an income.

Continue Your Education

When it comes to your education, subscribing to the life-long learning model never hurt anyone. What skills or certifications could you acquire to enhance your value or diversify your experience? Are there conferences, events or trainings that you could attend? What avenues can you explore to continue to pursue knowledge?

You don't necessarily have to stay within the barriers of your company. Look to related industries and fields. For example, many insurance brokers, financial planners, accountants and estate planning attorneys attend the same networking events or conferences to gain exposure to new ideas and developments. Some of the most creative and refreshing ideas can come when you're exposed to how other industries or businesses are doing things.

Keep Up with Industry Trends and Developments

What's the latest news in your company and industry? Are you aware of trends, revenue sources, and the overall market for your business or product? Do you know who your company's competitors are? Stay current by reading industry publications and understanding imminent changes or advances in technology or product design that are contributing to the bottom line. Be a resource!

Practice Being Essential

How can you make yourself indispensable to your employer or to your clients? Our generation has a reputation for being tech-savvy. As cliché as it may sound, take advantage of the fact that you catch on to technology trends quickly.

Could your company use a social media refresh (or rollout)? Could you volunteer to review the latest software products or CRMs that are meant to streamline your business and report back to the company on which make sense? If you own your own company, consider the ways you can provide indispensable value to your clients (without making yourself available 24/7). What are the small things that matter?

Always Build Relationships

It's not always about *who* you know. But when it comes to building your human capital, it could help to have a solid relationship with key members in your company or community. Who are you connected to professionally? Have you taken the time to invest in those relationships? Should you establish new ones?

Professional relationships aren't built overnight. They take time and commitment. If you're looking to connect with someone, ask questions about them and practice active listening. If you're seeking out input on a question, issue or project, be appreciative and respectful of the people providing you with their time and thoughts.

Identify Your Goals

If you were fired today, would you look for a similar position or make a change? Are you on the path to your dream job? Happiness is a factor when it comes to your human capital, as you're more likely to do your best work while in a job you enjoy.

Doing research, continuing to learn, building relationships, and being indispensable are easier to pursue when you're following your goals. If you're not currently in a position or industry that you enjoy, take some time to reflect upon where you'd like to be. Strategize for steps you could take that would get you there and begin to develop a plan to implement.

NEGOTIATE AN INCREASE

If you want to focus on one key strategy to boost your income, you need to learn how to negotiate. I've always been shocked by the people who just wait to be noticed at work. They work hard, take on additional projects, stay late and then get upset when they only receive the standard 2% to 3% annual pay increase. These employees feel gypped and ignored and inevitably end up looking for another job or consider switching industries. When I ask if they negotiated, I usually find they haven't.

Whether it's friends or clients that I talk to, it seems that negotiating your salary with your boss is as painful as a visit to the dentist. If you feel uncomfortable when it's time to ask for more, you're not alone. Many people – especially women – don't enjoy negotiating. Others simply don't know how. Either way, it's time to learn.

Asking for a raise when you've earned one is a serious investment in yourself, and managing your salary is a key part of achieving financial success. An average raise of $5,000 invested over 30 years with a 6% return can add a whopping $395,290 to your nest egg. Additionally, since future salary increases are often based on a percentage of your current salary, your salary will grow at a faster rate for the remainder of your career.

If you know that securing a raise is a smart financial move but still feel apprehensive about salary negotiation, use these four steps to overcome your apprehension and effectively negotiate your salary.

Do Your Best Work

When you do your best work and become essential to the organization's success, the salary negotiation process is much easier. As a key player, you can feel confident about your value to the company instead of worrying about job security. To make sure you understand what it takes to be the best you can be at your position, take the following steps:

- *Define your current job.* Work with your boss to establish baseline expectations for your current role. Make sure to bring your own ideas to the table, but solicit your boss's input.

- *Create a performance plan.* Work with your boss to define what success is for your role. What would provide so much value to your boss that a raise seems like a mere triviality?

- *Meet and exceed the expectations of the performance plan.* With a clearly defined path for success, you'll know exactly what you need to do to secure the raise you want. Make sure to capture moments of praise or achievement so you have great examples to share with your boss.

Prepare Yourself Before Any Meetings

In order to negotiate properly, there are a few things you'll want to bring with you to the meeting. First, you'll want to have a target number for the raise. Are you looking for a dollar amount or a percentage? Start by researching salary sites such as Payscale, Glassdoor or Salary. You can also talk with other people in the industry to gain insight into comparable figures for your role.

Remember that there's more to your compensation package than just your salary. Factor in items such as working from home benefits, extra vacations, potential performance bonuses and education funding. Consider if you're willing to take a lower salary for more flexible work hours or if the education benefits are a great way to enhance your ability to earn a higher income over the next few years.

Prepare and bring with you a list of achievements and accomplishments along with value you've added to the company. It's not enough to state that you deserve more money. Show, don't just tell.

I always recommend preparing for the conversation by enlisting a friend or partner to help you role-play the negotiation conversation. Have your friend push back at you in case you're met with resistance from your boss. If you feel apprehensive about walking into your boss's office and asking for more, knowing what words you'd like to say and how you'd like to say them will make a world of difference in feeling more comfortable during the negotiation.

Prepare Your Boss

Salary negotiations can be as uncomfortable for your boss as they are to you – and that's not personal. There are a lot of factors they have to consider in granting pay raises, and the decision may not be 100% in their hands.

If you have a regularly scheduled performance review, go to the meeting and knock it out of the park with your ample preparation. However, if your company is one of the 27% that doesn't evaluate performance regularly,, then ask for a meeting to evaluate your performance.[10]

Preparing your boss means avoid springing this conversation on them unexpectedly. Schedule a time to meet and talk. If you can, avoid scheduling this time around extremely busy periods in the office (when your manager may feel frazzled and stressed because of the

---

[10] http://www.salary.com/7-performance-review-myths/slide/4/

increased workload) or slow periods (when, after watching smaller profits come in, it may be harder to justify paying an employee more).

Conquer "No" and Other Negative Responses

I recommend always asking for slightly more than you'd be happy with as a pay increase in order to leave wiggle room for negotiation and a "meet-in-the-middle" mark. Don't be afraid to push back a little (but in a professional way). Always reiterate the value that you provide. Even with all of that, it's always possible that your boss will leave you with an outright "no." Here are a few questions to ask which will leave the door open for further conversation if you receive a negative response:

- If you don't think I'm at this pay rate yet, what do I need to do to get there?

- Would it be okay if I scheduled another performance and compensation review for us in three to six months?

- If you don't think a pay increase is an option at this time, would you be willing to [take advantage of some benefit, like working from home on Mondays]?

- Which areas would you like me to focus on improving over the next three to six months?

If you're really serious about increasing your compensation and your company is repeatedly resistant, or for whatever reason, you feel you won't be able to get ahead in your current position, consider moving to a different company. This shouldn't be your first choice of action, but it's something to consider if you're doing a great job but feel your opportunities for growth are limited.

Your ability to earn an income is your greatest asset and chances are you've worked hard to get where you are. It might seem like a lot of effort to continue investing in yourself and to go to this level of preparation to earn more, but this raise could translate into a significant amount of money over your working career. It's worth it to prepare adequately.

PUT A LITTLE HUSTLE IN YOUR LIFE

If career moves, salary negotiations or raises are not in the cards for you, you might want to consider launching a side hustle to earn more money.

When I prepared to launch Workable Wealth in 2013, I set the wheels in motion while I was still employed fulltime. I sought out paid writing opportunities as I knew that would help to build my online presence and portfolio. What evolved was a side hustle that is now a part of my ongoing business with Workable Wealth. In addition to one-on-one financial planning and coaching, I also get paid to write, speak and educate about money. This is a natural complement to the financial planning work I'm already doing (and is something I *really* enjoy doing), so it makes sense that it's now an income source for me.

Chances are you're really good at some thing(s) that you could monetize. You likely have amazing social media skills, are a fantastic chef, can speak four languages, do bookkeeping for your parent's business on the side, have a spectacular creative eye, are always the best dressed and know how to maximize your clothes for the dollar, have awesome negotiating skills, or any number of other skills, talents and knowledge that you could capitalize on and turn into a side hustle.

You are amazing at a lot of things. Take a minute to reflect on what you're usually complimented on by friends, family and coworkers. What skills or talents are people interested in of yours? What do people wish they could do that you *can* do? Those will likely be the areas where your side hustle will thrive.

Even if you don't have a particular skill in mind, there are options available to you. You can go online and provide virtual assistant services, create a course on Udemy, provide a service via Fivver, or sell items on eBay, Amazon or Etsy. You can go off line and babysit, tutor, walk dogs or housesit. You can even go more entrepreneurial and rent your home on Airbnb or become a driver for Uber or Lyft.

The goal with a side business is not to burn yourself out but to give yourself the opportunity to earn some extra cash that can go towards your financial goals while also doing something you enjoy. If the chances of you earning more at your current position are slim and you're in a place of wanting some extra money, dip your toe into the side hustle waters and see if you find something you love.

Money Move

Nobody will look out for you like you look out for you. Increasing your income and investing in yourself are important parts of securing your financial future.

Take time to complete these Money Moves:

- ☐ Head to Payscale, Salary or Glassdoor to review current salary averages for your position. Take note if there's room for an increase in your pay and determine what you'd like to earn.

- ☐ If you're self-employed, review your current pricing and determine if it's time to increase your product or service rates compared to your competition and the value of what you provide. Don't be afraid to charge your worth.

- ☐ Create a list of your experience, achievements and accolades as testament for a salary or pricing increase.

- ☐ Enlist a friend or partner and start role-playing conversations you'll have with your boss or clients/customers about increases.

- ☐ Make a list of three ways you can invest in your ability to earn an income this year and add the courses, events or trainings you want to attend to your calendar. Commit to implementing at least one lesson or change in your role or company after each training to ensure you're taking action on what you learn.

- ☐ Be prepared to receive "No" as an answer and set the stage for future conversations and timing

Chapter 9:

CONQUER YOUR REAL-LIFE MONEY ISSUES

"We need to accept that we won't always make the right decisions, that we'll screw up royally sometimes -- understanding that failure is not the opposite of success, it's part of success."
~ Arianna Huffington

Up until this point, you've taken all the steps needed to build your own financial plan! You've set goals, created a cash flow plan to help you use your money with intention, checked in on your financial health, created a plan to knock out debt, learned how to manage your credit and your investments, and put the protection needed to cover your most valuable assets into place.

But what about the questions that remain? You know, the *real-life* situations that you face on a day-to-day basis? I haven't forgotten about those! This chapter is dedicated towards walking you through some of the money questions that still remain for you, such as:

- How should I tackle my student loans?
- Should I rent or own a home?
- How should I handle extra money I receive?
- How do I build my own money team?
- Should I take this new job?
- How do I handle financial frenemies?

Feel free to read the chapter in full or skip through to the questions that apply to your life only. Each question will have a page or two dedicated to it as an overview.

HOW SHOULD I TACKLE MY STUDENT LOANS?

Are you stressed about your student loans? Wondering if you're on the right track for repayment? You're not alone. According to the non-profit organization American Student Assistance, about 20 million people attend college annually. Twelve million of those people borrow money each year to cover the expenses associated with their higher education.[11] That's in addition to the existing 37 million people who have outstanding student loans. It's no wonder people are stressed.

Whether you're about to embark on a pay-down strategy or you've been paying down your loan balances for years, here is an overview of options and considerations that may help you determine if you're on the right path.

How to Inventory Your Student Loans

To gain access to an overview of all of your student loans, you'll need to take a few steps. For private student loans, review your credit report, where you'll find a list of each outstanding loan. For federal student loans, you'll want to access the National Student Loan Data System. Visit NSLDS.ed.gov and click the Financial Aid Review button. You'll then need to enter the following:

- Your Social Security number
- The first two letters of your last name
- Your date of birth
- Your PIN (get it at pin.ed.gov)

---

[11] http://www.asa.org/policy/resources/stats/

You'll see a summary page and can click the blue numbers in the far left column to find more details on each loan. Click "My Student Data Download" to download a file with all your important details.

Options for Federal Student Loan Repayment

The programs below each have their own guidelines and requirements (or minimums) that you need to meet.

If your income is reasonable in relation to your student loan balance, you may want to consider sticking with the *Standard Repayment Plan,* where your payments are a fixed amount per month for up to ten years and you pay the least amount of interest. You can also look at the *Graduated Repayment Plan,* where your payments will be lower to start and will increase every few years for up to ten years. You'll pay more interest in this option than in the standard repayment plan.

If you need to have more affordable loan payments, consider the *Extended Repayment Plan,* which allows smaller fixed or graduated payments, and lets you pay off your loan in up to 25 years. There's also a *Pay As You Earn* plan designed to help students who have just graduated and are entering a tough job market where wages are lower. If you qualify, this program caps monthly loan payments at 10% of discretionary income. This option can help ease cash flow strain for individuals who qualify, but be aware that this will stretch out the amount of time you're paying back your loan and may increase the overall interest you'll pay.

Income Based Repayment (IBR) is another option, which aims to keep monthly payments affordable. Payment caps are based on how much money you make and the size of your household but are limited to 15% of discretionary income. Any remaining unpaid balances after 25 years may be forgiven, but note you will be taxed on the amount forgiven.

How to Start Paying Down Your Student Loans

Here's a process you can follow to determine how you'll repay what you owe.

Saving vs. Paying Off Debt

Chances are you know saving your money is just as important as paying off your debt. But how do you know how much to save or what you should be saving for or how to save and pay off your debt? It can be difficult to prioritize.

You should put creating a cash cushion of about $1,000 at the top of your financial to-do list. A small emergency fund can help you get through unexpected situations without pushing you further into debt. If you have bigger goals, look down the road for a longer period. The standard repayment period on student loans is ten years, and you probably don't want to wait that long to save for a house or for a wedding.

You need to find a way to balance paying off your student loans with saving, if that's the case. You can re-evaluate your budget to see if you can cut any costs or lessen some expenses. Be critical about what's truly a need and what falls under the "wants" category. Also consider earning extra money to fund savings with a separate income stream. This allows you to make progress in a number of areas instead of being limited to just one financial priority.

What Are Your Interest Rates?

The higher your interest rate, the more money you're paying to borrow money. Additionally, the longer your repayment term, the more you'll end up paying over the life of the loan.

Some people believe in paying the minimum if your interest rates are around 2.2% or lower, because saving and investing your money could get you a better return on your money. But that assumes you actually save your money! If your interest rates are on the higher end — around 5% or more —prioritize paying them off. You don't want to pay more money toward interest if you don't have to.

Making Extra Payments

The more you can pay towards your student loans, the less you'll be paying towards interest. This allows you to chip away at the principal balance of your loan. You don't necessarily have to pay extra all the time, or only during your regular payment, either. Pay more when you can, even if it's just once or twice a year.

What if You Can't Afford Payments?

Many graduates have six figures in student loan debt and no way to repay it. If that describes your situation and you're stressing about affording your student loan payments, there are a few options to consider.

If you have federal loans, look to the flexible income-based repayment options listed above. Call your loan servicer and explain the situation you're in. They might be able to recommend a specific repayment plan to look into.

If you're struggling to make payments on your loans, you may also be eligible for deferment, which is a temporary period where you don't have to make payments and interest doesn't accrue on subsidized loans. (Interest does accrue on unsubsidized loans.) Forbearance is similar to deferment, except interest continues accruing on all of your loans during the time you don't have to make payments. Not having to make payments gives you a chance to get back on your feet and to begin managing your cash flow better.

Getting your federal loans forgiven, discharged or canceled is possible, but only in select circumstances. These options mean you no longer owe anything on your student loans.

Unfortunately, private loans don't come with the variety of repayment plans federal loans do, but many lenders are willing to work with borrowers by granting them forbearance periods. If you need help, pick up the phone and call your loan servicer and see what they can do for you.

Refinancing or consolidating are two options to look into as well. The purpose of refinancing your student loans is to improve your terms (to lower your interest rate, for example). The purpose of consolidating your loans is to make it easier to pay them. If you owe money to seven different lenders, consolidating them rolls them all into one easy payment.

SHOULD I RENT OR OWN A HOME?

For many of us, the great American dream still revolves around home ownership. Building equity and saving money on rent seem to be at the top of the list whether you're single or married. Here are important considerations to review before making a choice to buy.

(If you're paired off, ensure you have a detailed conversation or two with your partner about this topic. Share this chapter with them and discuss together.)

Where Do You See Yourself in Five Years?

Do you see yourself getting married, changing careers, or moving out of state in the next few years? What about incurring large expenses such as having children or buying a new car? Consider your current job and the stability associated with it. Can you expect to be there for the next few years?

Although you may feel the need to purchase a home now, consider renting until the dust settles from any big transitions you may face in the next three to five years and you have more stability. While you may be able to sell a home that you purchased just a few years ago, being faced with having to make a quick decision or sale could hurt you financially.

Can You Afford *All* Expenses Associated with a Home?

Whether you're using a gift, loan from parents, or savings to cover the down payment on a home, it's important to maintain an adequate emergency fund for repairs and to factor items such as monthly maintenance, homeowner's association dues, property taxes, and insurance into your budget. Be sure to consider if you need to make repairs, paint, purchase furniture, appliances or fixtures, and factor in closing and moving costs into your expenses. A good rule of thumb to consider is that no more than 28% of your gross monthly income should be used to pay for PITI (principal, interest, taxes and insurance). Do your research and understand *all* costs that go into home ownership, from the initial purchase to the ongoing upkeep to the potential changes in your taxes and insurance and even your mortgage if you don't have a fixed rate.

How's Your Credit?

Your credit score plays a big role in terms of the type of financing and mortgage rate you'll qualify for. If you haven't checked it in the past year, use a website such as annualcreditreport.com or Credit Karma to get some insight into where you stand. Keep in mind that your existing debt load could cut into your ability to qualify for a mortgage.

What Does the Local Real Estate Market Look Like?

To start, does the location work for you? Before buying in a location of your desire, first consider items such as an added commute to work and increased cost of living for items like gas and groceries. Step back and look at the prices of homes in the market. Are they on the rise, holding steady or declining? What type of inventory is available in your desired community? Look back a few years and see what's transpired over time and understand where you may be buying in the "cycle."

Is Your Lifestyle Conducive to Home Ownership?

Sit down and think about your day-to-day life as well as your weekends. Are you constantly on the go, visiting family and friends, traveling and experiencing the next greatest thing, or are you happy staying in and relaxing at home? Understand that there is a time and financial cost associated with home ownership in terms of maintenance, upkeep and repairs. Are you willing to do it yourself, or will you factor in additional expenses for items like gardening and pool cleaning? How will you handle home repairs as an owner instead of a renter? Expectations will be different and your new neighborhood may come with some strict landscaping requirements depending on the type of HOA you're faced with. Ensure that you're up for maintaining things yourself or that you have a plan in place if you'd like to outsource.

If you want to crunch the numbers in more detail, check out "buy vs. rent" calculators online. If you're ready to start pricing out homes, use a website such as Zillow or Trulia to get an idea of home prices and inventory in your ideal neighborhood.

HOW SHOULD I HANDLE EXTRA INCOME?

If you're like me, receiving a rare cash bonus, big tax refund, or any type of large cash gift inspires visions of new clothes and exotic trips. Before we start spending our newfound cash, however, it's important to take a step back and evaluate how we can make the most of this extra money.

While this shouldn't be an excuse for mindless splurging, it doesn't mean you can't have a little fun. By having a plan in place before you receive the money, you can make progress on financial goals and give yourself a small treat. Consider these five ideas to put your cash to use:

Tackle Debts First

It might not sound too exciting, but using the money to accelerate your debt repayment is a smart move. If you want to make the most of it, put the money towards your debt with the highest interest rate. Paying off those debts as soon as possible means you pay less in interest in the long run.

Set Up an Emergency Fund and Save Up for Irregular Expenses

If you don't already have an emergency fund, use this money to start one, or to top yours off so you can check the box on having this goal fully funded. If your emergency fund is stocked, consider setting aside the money for other specific or irregular expenses that are difficult to budget for, like car maintenance, veterinary bills or home maintenance.

Max Out Your 401(k) or IRA

You may already contribute to a retirement account on a regular basis, but you could use extra income to do more. Using this money to fund your retirement through a 401(k), Roth IRA, or a retirement account for self-employed workers is an excellent way to contribute to your future and take advantage of that oh-so-important topic we've talked about called compound interest.

Invest in Yourself

We discussed how important your human capital and ability to earn an income is in the previous chapter. Investing in yourself is a great way to increase your earning capacity.

Use your cash to invest in yourself by taking a class, continuing your education, or adding to your skill set. If you possess the drive to learn and improve, you may even be able to market your newly acquired knowledge or skill as a side hustle to earn more money and increase your ROI (return on investment).

Enjoy a Splurge (But Make Sure It's the Right Kind)

Yes – you can splurge! A little. Money can allow you to build security and stability, but it can also buy some happiness when you put it to good use: spending on experiences and relationships.

Use your bonus to take yourself on a fun trip you might otherwise skip or go to an event that you've always wanted to attend. Spread out your splurge and plan for one fancy date night a month for the next three months. Travel to visit a friend or family member you haven't seen in a while.

Spending money isn't a bad thing, and you don't have to squirrel away every last cent of your extra cash, but practice mindful spending and work to align it with what you really value.

Can't Choose Among These Options?

Choosing the "best" avenue for extra cash can be a challenge. That's because your best option will be unique to you and your financial goals, wants and needs. You may have debts to tackle, an emergency fund to top up, *and* a camping trip you've been wanting to take.

Don't feel as if you have to choose among them. Instead, consider dividing your money to go towards each. Work in percentages to address multiple priorities and goals. Maybe you can put 50% to debt, 30% towards savings and use 20% to splurge. Ultimately, the best use for your money will depend on your individual needs and goals. Choosing one of these ways to put your extra money to good use will help you get started in the right direction.

WHO DO I NEED ON MY MONEY TEAM?

When it comes to building wealth, it pays to have a money team. As Thomas Stanley, author of *The Millionaire Next Door*, found in his research, the best wealth accumulators usually assemble a team of advisors when making important financial decisions.

If you want to build and preserve your wealth, you need a money team, too. When you're talking about something as important as your financial security, it's crucial to get it right. With the right professionals on your side, you'll have peace of mind – and end up with more in the bank.

Financial Planner

A financial planner, or financial advisor, will help you look at the entire picture of your financial life. A planner will help you figure out how to accomplish your financial dreams by establishing goals, evaluating your current money situation, and creating a plan to help you get there.

Even if you like to manage your own money, it's helpful to have a trained eye to look for opportunities and risks you might not see yourself. Sometimes the most valuable thing a financial planner can do for you is to prevent you from making emotional decisions. This person can help with money management, investing advice, estate planning, insurance planning, business planning, and more. They'll help you pull together the big picture of your financial life, and they'll work with the other members of your money team to help you implement your financial plan. I practice what I preach in this area and have a financial planner myself. It helps to have a second set of eyes on our finances and ensures there's a neutral third party for tough money choices my husband and I may need to make. Doctors need their own doctors and financial planners need their own financial planners, too.

When choosing a planner, make sure you look for someone who is fee-only (and won't make a commission off of an investment or product they're trying to sell you) and is willing to work as your fiduciary (in your best interest). They should also have the CFP® designation.

Attorney

No money team is complete without the help of a good attorney. An important task for your attorney will be to create an estate plan, which will include a will, living trust and power of attorney. These documents help friends and family navigate settling your estate according to your wishes. If you have children that are still dependent on you financially, this is extremely important. You want to make sure your children will be taken care of by a person of your choosing.

Many of us will want a trust to protect our assets, and this is when having an expert can really help. For example, if you're a doctor with a risk for a malpractice suit, some states have more favorable laws than others. When it comes to estate planning, it's wise to have an expert. Depending on your investments and your financial situation, you may call on an attorney on a regular basis. They can help review business deals, real estate purchases, and more.

Accountant

Even if you consider yourself to be good with math, you'll still want an accountant on your team. Many high-income earners put more towards taxes than they do towards any other expense. With so much money at stake, it makes financial sense to work with an expert on tax strategy. Your accountant can help you prepare your taxes, offer appropriate tax shelter recommendations, manage depreciation schedules, and more.

Insurance Broker

The more your wealth grows, the more you have at stake. An insurance broker will help determine the right insurance products to help you manage this risk.

Insurance products can be complex. Take disability insurance as an example. There's a wide range of products and prices available.

Since disability insurance depends on your occupation, one person might not even qualify for certain policies. An experienced broker will help you navigate the insurance marketplace.

Your financial planner and insurance broker will work together to help you create a comprehensive insurance plan.

Additional Team Members for Entrepreneurs

As a business owner, you'll need a few more people on your money team. For one, you'll want a seasoned attorney that understands your business. Depending on your business, you may need to consult multiple attorneys, such as a contract lawyer, patent lawyer, and so on. You might also benefit from working with a bookkeeper. A bookkeeper will help you track your expenses and profits so you can make better money decisions on a daily basis.

SHOULD I TAKE THIS JOB OFFER?

It's happened to many of us in today's economy. We're waiting to make that next big career move or hoping to transition to a new field, and in our earnest and eagerness we say "YES!" to the first opportunity that drops in our lap. I'm all about walking through doors that open for you, but before you take that leap, there are some money questions you should answer first.

Wages: Is the position hourly or salaried? Is there an option for a bonus or possible commission? Ensure you understand what portion of your income will be guaranteed and fixed versus what's variable. Work to create a household spending plan on the new amounts. It's important that you understand how your new income will affect your spending and goals.

Vacation, Sick Leave and Paid Time Off: Life happens and you want to have time to enjoy it. Find out about company-provided vacation days and paid time off for doctor's appointments or unexpected events. Knowing what comes with the package can help you to better navigate future vacation plans and any issues that may take you away from work. You'll have a clearer understanding of what these events may cost you in terms of time or lost wages.

Insurance Benefits (Life, Health, Disability): This is an important area to ask about. Health insurance, whether single or with a family, can take up a significant chunk of your monthly income. If possible, gauge what the company offers ahead of time and ask about the average cost of coverage for employees in order to compare to what you're currently paying. In addition, benefits such as life insurance or disability coverage can help to supplement outside benefits you may have or provide enough coverage to where you may not need to spend out of pocket for these items.

Retirement Plans and Options: Saving for your future self is a priority no matter where you're working. Ask about company retirement plan options, such as a 401(k) and determine if there's a company match (which is free money!). If there isn't a 401(k) option, you'll need to look outside to setting up your own Traditional or Roth Individual Retirement Account. In addition to retirement plans, determine if there are stock options or any other company incentives.

Performance Reviews: Although not the highest-ranking question, having clarity around company expectations for performance and salary reviews will help you to determine whether this is a company you can expect structure and streamlined growth with (assuming you meet the company criteria), or if it's one where you'll need to push the needle forward and proactively ask for reviews.

Continuing Education Opportunities: Are you in a position that requires you to hold a license and take annual continuing education credits? Will your new employer share in or cover the costs for you to maintain these designations? In addition, are there any types of professional development or educational reimbursements for courses you take to advance your skills within your new position? Understand if these are expenses that will need to be maintained on your own or if the company invests in its employees under this option. This can help you to answer questions around paying for an advanced degree, maintaining licenses, enhancing your leadership skills and more.

Company Culture: Company culture may not seem like a money-related question, but you'll need to understand work hours, flexibility, and whether it's a family-oriented company. Knowing whether you'll be able to step away for a few hours one afternoon when your child is sick or if you'll need to secure some type of paid care is important to factor into family expenses.

In addition, if you're taking on a demanding job that will have you away from home or neglecting personal care, these are items that could factor into higher costs for health care for stress-related issues. Evaluate your current lifestyle and ensure you understand the changes, if any, you'll face when joining a new company.

HOW DO I HANDLE FINANCIAL FRENEMIES?

According to Wikipedia, a 'frenemy' is a combination of "friend" and "enemy" that can refer to either an enemy pretending to be a friend or someone who really *is* a friend but is also a rival.

While it's highly unlikely that your friends are intentional financial frenemies, they may be unintentionally wreaking havoc on your spending and your money. Here are six statements to look out for and how to get back on track:

"Can you spot me? I'll get you next time." It occasionally happens that our friends forget their wallet at home or don't have the cash on hand to cover a bill. Once in a while is okay. Once a month, however, is not. If your friend is in the habit of mooching off of you, it may be time to sit down and set some boundaries on spending. Of course you want to have a good time with your friends, but that doesn't mean you need to foot the bill. Create a strategy to curb loans in the future, suggest that your friend gets financially organized, and don't be afraid to say "no."

"You should TOTALLY buy that. You deserve it." I admit, I've told my friends that they deserve things. Like a raise, a better boyfriend, and from time to time a splurge on themselves. However, who am I to tell them it's okay to splurge when I have no idea what their finances look like? If you're being told this, it doesn't translate into you having the funds to cover the purchase. Step back and evaluate or give yourself a 24-hour cooling-off period before making the buy. If you don't have the money on hand, what are you willing to give up for the next few months to cover the expense?

"You got a $50 gift card from your boss for the holidays? Can you believe I got a $3,000 bonus!?" Just when you're feeling appreciated by others and like you've scored, a friend comes along to one-up you. It's hard not to feel bad or compare in these situations, but your best bet may be to ignore the comments. You recognize that you have worked hard and you deserve the opportunity to feel good about it. If it is truly a bad and consistent habit from a good friend, having a conversation about how the money comments are making you feel may be a good place to start.

"How big was your raise? How much did you pay for that?" (and other prying questions). While talking finances is okay, know that if someone who isn't your financial planner is asking you questions like this, it may be for a comparison game they're playing with themselves. When disclosing information to family members or friends, be aware that this information may be shared with others. If you're comfortable sharing and making your numbers public, ensure it's with a trusted source. If you're uncomfortable, deflect the questions with general answers such as "My raise? They met what I was asking for, which makes me feel like a recognized and valued team member."

"Must be nice that you can afford that house (car, shoes, purse, restaurant, etc.)" There's a little green-eyed monster in all of us, but if you find that you're feeling guilty for certain purchases that are well within your budget or find yourself playing down some of your possessions in order to make others feel better, that's defeating the purpose of allowing yourself to enjoy your money and using it to live a life you value. While there's a balance with showing off, feeling guilty and playing down expenses won't help you or your friend. The best way to neutralize the situation is to simply address the comment by saying something like, "Thanks. I'm really enjoying the new place."

"It's just one dinner (one drink, one vacation, etc.)" Even though your friends know you're trying to save money, they can't help but to encourage you to come out "just this once." In times like these, it's hard to say no, especially when there's a genuine fear of missing out that's going on in our society. If you're not the type to miss out, ensure that you set aside some money for "impulse" spending in your budget each month. This will allow you to have the funds on hand for a random night out. Or, instead of going out, suggest cheaper alternatives, such as game or movie nights, potlucks or lunch dates, in order to get in quality time with friends and still save money.

Money Move

Life happens and you have questions that need answering.

Take time to complete these Money Moves:

- ☐ Write a list of the financial issues you're facing and questions you have in your financial life that may still be unanswered.

- ☐ Schedule time (perhaps an hour a week) over the next three or four weeks to research each question and determine the best path for moving forward.

- ☐ If you're unsure of where to begin on answering your outstanding questions, consider scheduling a consultation with a financial planner who has experience working with clients like you who can help you create a plan.

Chapter 10:

IT'S YOUR FINANCIAL LIFE

"The difference between successful people and others is how long they spend time feeling sorry for themselves." ~ Barbara Corcoran

MONEY ≠ HAPPINESS

Money does not equal a straight path to happiness. You could have $5,000,000 in the bank or $5,000, but either way, there's no guarantee for peace of mind.

I've talked to people who are earning $300,000 per year who don't feel confident or educated in what they're doing with their money. I've talked with people earning $50,000 per year who feel the same. Clarity and confidence around your finances does not happen overnight, no matter what your income is or what your bank account balances are. If you read this book and expected someone to do the work for you in fixing things, you might be a little underwhelmed. As with all of my clients, I can take the information, organize it for you, create a plan of action and hold you accountable to implementing it, but you have to do the work. You have to be willing to make the changes. I can't change you. I can't make you do it.

There is shame, anxiety, discomfort and stress galore in the world when it comes to money. If you're beating yourself up because you haven't made the right decisions in the past, feel like you should be much further along than you are now, hate that you're the one making all the financial decisions in your relationship, or just really, really don't like numbers, I'd encourage you to put some concrete details around those fears. If you think you should be further along, just where exactly do you think you should be? Own a home? Have more in the bank? Less debt? What is it that you think you "should" have? And who are you comparing yourself to or what are you basing these assumptions on?

I've talked to so many people who are wrapped up in a shame spiral or feel intense discomfort and anxiety when it comes to money that they simply cannot focus on moving forward. They're too busy beating themselves up or burying themselves under all the things that must change or happen in order to get to this imaginary place of "better" in their lives.

It's time to stop the cycle!

LIFE IS A JUNGLE

If I've learned anything in life, it's that rarely do things go as planned. The reason we have plans and create lists of action items for ourselves is so we can maintain some control when things do go awry. Your money and your financial plan *will* go off course. Multiple times. You will change jobs, lose jobs, get bonuses, have kids, sell homes, move, get sick, lose family members, make more money, start a business, get promotions, and a whole lot more over the course of your life.

The reason you went through this book is to give yourself the education you need to get through those changes. Not only do you *need* a financial education, but you *deserve* one! Your life is changing every second of every day. You don't have time to feel anxious about money, nor should you feel insecure about asking the questions that you need answers to in order to rid yourself of that anxiety.

Life is a jungle, but here's the catch: It's that way for *everyone*. You are not alone in feeling uneasy. Rarely are people born with a financial education or expertise in hand. If you want out of the jungle, you have to do the work to find your way out. But it doesn't have to be that hard.

ORGANIZATION IS KEY

This book was laid out in a way that gives you the tools to build your own financial plan and a roadmap out of the financial jungle you may have been in.

You should now have goals, a spending plan, a debt pay-down plan, an idea of your net worth, and knowledge of where to start with investing and the types of financial protections you need in your life.

The Money Moves at the end of each chapter laid out the steps you need to take to get you to this point. If you're here and you know that you still have things to take care of, open up a Word or Excel document and make one big Action Checklist for yourself and note two or three items you'll accomplish each month.

I have clients start with the easier tasks, like signing up for Mint or You Need a Budget. Since it takes time to begin analyzing the numbers there, I then immediately move to opening up separate emergency fund, home-buying, and travel savings accounts, and setting up ongoing monthly contributions into each. This should take about 30 minutes and, boom, you've made progress in getting your money organized!

From there, it's time to implement the debt pay-down plan that has been laid out, starting with moving all extra funds to whichever balance will be paid off first. Next, the focus turns to investments and making the necessary adjustments to get on track with 401(k)s, Roth IRAs, and so on. Finally, the items that require more time and additional analyzing and research come into play. We choose the correct life and disability insurance policies and put estate planning documents in place.

Add each of these items to your checklist if you haven't already completed them and also include things like pulling your credit report and your Social Security benefits estimate (which you can obtain online). Put the Action Checklist on your refrigerator and make a note on your calendar to have monthly money dates with yourself to review progress on your finances.

MONEY DATES TO STAY ON TRACK

Even if you have a full plan for your money laid out and implemented, periodic money dates are essential to your financial success. You can't manage what you don't measure, and these dates provide the perfect space for you to sit down on your own or with your partner to examine all aspects of your finances to ensure you're on the right track.

Use this sample agenda to make sure you hit the important points and stay focused. Make tweaks to ensure your specific situation is covered.

Schedule a time: Set a recurring monthly appointment on your calendar. Make it the third Friday of each month, the first day of each month, every other payday, or whatever works for you. Just ensure you're sticking to it. This is a priority and will set the stage for you to be less stressed in the days ahead by knowing you're on track or have readjusted. Delaying only heightens the anxiety of what you'll have to face. The more you have your head in the game and the more consistent you are with checking in, the better things will get over time.

Gather what you need: Before sitting down to review, make sure you have everything you need. Grab your laptop so you can check in with online accounts or review everything on Mint, your account statements, your list of goals and the progress points on each of them that designate periodic financial wins, your monthly budget (for the past month and the upcoming month), and anything else that helps you track your personal finances.

Take care of any necessary tasks: Pay any bills that are due, update account information as necessary, and schedule anything that you need to take care of (like calling a service provider to ask for a discount or scheduling a meeting with your accountant). If you have anything that needs to be organized and updated, like receipts or other paperwork to file, do it now.

Review the previous month: Start evaluating your finances by checking out your activity from the previous month. Examine every angle at your budget. Look at:

- Total income for the month.
- Amounts automatically deducted (retirement contributions, taxes, health insurance, etc.).
- How much was spent on necessary expenses (mortgage or rent, utilities, gas and groceries).
- How much was spent on discretionary purchases (entertainment, meals out and shopping).
- How much was contributed to debt repayment (if applicable).
- How much was contributed to savings.
- Your income minus your expenses – was there a surplus?

Check your accounts: Quickly review your online accounts, including checking, savings, credit cards, loan balances, bills, retirement savings, and so on. Look through the last month's activity to ensure there are no errors and to make sure your budget reflects the same activity as your accounts do.

Track everything: Conclude analyzing your finances by tracking everything. Include savings, debts, investments and income. Then calculate your net worth using the sheet you created in Chapter 5. All these steps allow you to see the details *and* the big picture on your finances.

Reflect on the numbers: Once you have the most recent numbers, take a moment to talk about or review them. Did you overspend in any of your budget categories? Why? Is there anything you can do next month that will help you cut back on costs and spending? Or maybe you had a budget surplus. Can you identify how you were able to save more than you expected? How can you do that again next month? Be sure to transfer that money over to savings or debt repayments as well!

Examine financial goals: Next, look at how these numbers affected your current goals. If you were able to put another payment towards your debt, look at how you're chipping away at the total. If you contributed to retirement, note how much is in your nest egg now. Keep track of these numbers and use them to track your progress during future money dates.

Review your goals: When you record how much progress you've made, see if it's time to celebrate a financial win. If it is, make plans to do so! If not, take a moment to reflect on your goals and why they're important to you. You can stay motivated by reminding yourself why you're working hard to build up your emergency savings so you have the stability to try something like starting your own business or taking a year to travel the world.

If paired off, check in with each other: Now is also a good time to check in not just with the numbers but also with your partner. Make sure you give one another a moment to talk about thoughts and opinions on the state of your finances. Share any suggestions for improvements or express if something's bothering you.

Adjust: If you need to make changes in the next month, make a plan to do so.

Keep in mind that if you don't have an accountability buddy, now may be the time to get one. When you have one, never try to keep secrets or hide a money issue. Working towards your biggest financial goals takes time and hard work. By taking action, you're making excellent progress towards working your wealth and accomplishing what's most important to you.

CELEBRATE YOUR WINS

The same year I decided to launch Workable Wealth, my husband also decided to transition out of his active-duty service with the U.S. Navy. We also thought it would be a good idea to get on the baby-making train and try to sell our home. What transpired was a *huge* shift in income, discovering our need to go through infertility treatments and incur *a lot* of unexpected expenses, and some really in-depth conversations about our priorities and goals.

There was a whole lot of change on the horizon, but what helped us to get through it was to make it a point of celebrating our financial wins to continue to make money something enjoyable and pleasant in our lives. Here are the five W's of financial wins and how you can implement them in your home:

Who: YOU, of course.

What: A financial win occurs when you meet a predetermined point on a goal. For example, for every $1,500 we add to our household net worth (actual savings, not market related), we allow ourselves $100 to spend on our "wants" list. This is a way for us to pause, recognize what we've accomplished, and have a small celebration in the name of our progress.

Financial wins can be unique to your situation – either a percent of goal funded, a certain amount stashed away, an amount of debt paid down, and so on. The thing to keep in mind when drafting your wins is to make them something you're *working* towards. Don't go too easy on yourself by saving $200 and spending $100, but don't be too restrictive either. Decide what works best for you, recognize the delay it may create in reaching your goals, and then implement and stick to it. Don't feel guilty for celebrating your wins if you're confident that you're working hard towards your goals. Taking pause to applaud ourselves is what keeps us motivated to push on.

When: There's no better time to start celebrating your financial success than immediately. We all have financial goals we're working towards. Take ten minutes right now to think about the actions you're already taking in your life to get financially organized. Now, add in a time to celebrate your progress intermittently with a small amount, whether it's $20 for a week's worth of lattes or $100 for a date night or gift purchase. Do what makes sense for you.

Where: We keep our "wants" list right on our refrigerator. Pale green paper and a purple marker do the trick of making it noticeable. Some of the items are $15 and some are $200 or $300. Some have been purchased and are crossed out and some are waiting until it's their turn.

Why: I'm a financial planner. I recognize that if we kept stashing away as much money as possible, we'll meet our goals at a faster rate. However, it's not just about the destination for us. It's about the journey. The fun for us comes in celebrating along the way. 25%, 50%, 75% goal funding is a time for us to take pause – and $100, if we'd like, and buy something we've been looking forward to.

Financial wins are something everyone and anyone can celebrate. The key is to ensure you're at the point of celebrating a financial win first.

IT'S YOUR FINANCIAL LIFE

You work hard for your money and now it's time to make your money work for you. You have the tools and resources you need to take control of your finances and if you've completed this book, you're hopefully well on your way.

Remember that there is no one clear definition of wealth. If you're going to work your wealth, recognize that what it means to you will likely be very different from what it means for your friends and family. Understanding what exactly it is that you want in your life, and the type of experiences or things you want included, will help you stay invested.

It's up to you to throw away your anxiety around money once and for all. Remember to be kind to yourself, break down big steps into smaller ones, have monthly money dates, celebrate your wins, grab an accountability partner, and take the twists, turns, and ups and downs in stride along the way. Now that you have a plan, you're prepared to work your wealth in the best way for *you*. Enjoy the ride!

Appendix

Below are the resources, websites and calculators that were mentioned in each chapter in addition to those available at www.workyourwealthbook.com.

Chapter 2: Put Your Money Where Your Heart Is
Mint (www.mint.com)
You Need a Budget (www.youneedabudget.com)
QuickBooks (www.quickbooks.intuit.com)
Quicken (www.quicken.com)
Strong Inside Out (www.stronginsideout.com)

t.com)

rb

rs/mortgages/amortiza-

Check-Up

Ally Bank (www.ally.com)

Vanguard (www.vanguard.com)
Scottrade (www.scottrade.com)
E*TRADE (www.etrade.com)

Chapter 7: Protect You're A$$ets
Life Happens Life Insurance Calculator: (http://www.lifehappens.org/ insurance-overview/life-insurance/calculate-your-needs/)

Chapter 8: Optimize Your Income
Payscale (www.payscale.com)
Glassdoor (www.glassdoor.com)
Salary.com (www.salary.com)
Udemy (www.udemy.com)
eBay (www.ebay.com)
Amazon (www.amazon.com)
Etsy (www.etsy.com)
Fivver (www.fivver.com)
Airbnb (www.airbnb.com)
Uber (www.uber.com)
Lyft (www.lyft.com)

Chapter 9: Conquer Your Real-Life Money Issues
AnnualCreditReport (www.annualcreditreport.com)
Credit Karma (www.creditkarma.com)
Zillow (www.zillow.com)
Trulia (www.trulia.com)

Chapter 10: It's Your Financial Life
Mint (www.mint.com)
You Need a Budget (www.youneedabudget.com)
Social Security (www.ssa.gov)

Acknowledgments

Where does one start with saying "Thank you"? This might be the hardest part of writing a book!

This book wouldn't be in existence without the support and push from my amazing husband, Brian, who has been my number one fan throughout the whole process of becoming an entrepreneur. I love you more than you'll ever know.

To Ellie, it is my goal in life to make you proud. You won't be able to read this for quite some time, but know that I'll strive every day to be the best Mama to you that I can.

To Mom and Dad, thank you for showing me what hard work looks like and what it means to put family first. You've always supported me no matter what crazy adventure I'm embarking on and have always pushed me to reach for the stars. Thank you for teaching me so much.

To Theresa and Sammi, I wouldn't be who I am without the pieces of our stories and memories that I carry with me at all times. Thank you for always making me smile and being just a phone call away.

To my sister from another mister, Andrea Fowler. Can I say you complete me here? 100% not sure where I'd be without you. I couldn't ask for a better person to call my best friend.

To Nida. "What's the worst that can happen?" It was your string of text messages that gave the last push I needed to make this leap. We've come a long way since the days in the Groves. I'm so lucky to have you.

To my extended family full of crazy Italians and to my fun and loving in-laws, thank you for being the most supportive and loving people I could ask for, for always checking in, helping me take a break when needed, and in the case of the world's best mother-in-law, red-penning the heck out of this book so that it's (mostly) grammatically correct.

To my friends who have pushed, encouraged, challenged, supported and loved me through it all. You are amazing and I love you all: Joseph Ferro, Lisa Hinz, Nicole Phelps, Lindsey Fraytes, Lindsey Arledge, Ashley Sowles, Stephanie Cisar, Colleen D'Agostino and Marybeth Kneussl. To those not listed, know that you're in my heart and I'm so thankful for each of you.

To the FPHackers (Sophia Bera, Alan Moore & Eric Roberge). I couldn't have kicked off this journey with a better crew and can't believe how far we've come. Thank you for the reality checks every Monday for the past two years. Lord knows I needed them.

To Kali Hawlk. Your support and guidance throughout this whole process has been invaluable. I am so thankful to have you as a part of this project and can't say thank you enough for all of your work.

To the HoyleCohen crew (Karen Neal, Rachel Luken, Joe Cohen, Mark Delfino, Ellen Sawyer, Vanessa Wieliczko). Thanks for your endless support, guidance, mentoring, pushing, challenging and more since you were introduced into my life.

Thank you to Melody Christian for being amazing to work with and for making this book (cover included) absolutely beautiful. Thank you to Dana Malstaff for going through the trenches ahead of me and sharing your feedback and experience with me.

Most of all, thank YOU for grabbing this book and taking a step in educating yourself about your finances. It is my dream to make financial education and planning around your money fun, afford-able and accessible for the next generation and with your help, we're making it happen!

About the Author

Mary Beth Storjohann, CFP® is the Founder of Workable Wealth, specializing in financial planning for Gen Y & Gen X. She is an author, speaker, and financial coach working on a national level to help individuals and couples in their 20s, 30s, and 40s make smart, educated decisions with their money. Her first book, *Work Your Wealth: 9 Steps to Making Smarter Choices With Your Money*, provides clear-cut guidance on the money moves you can make to improve your financial situation right now.

As a speaker, she delivers captivating, authentic, and direct professional insights surrounding a variety of personal finance topics.

As a coach with over 12 years of experience, she applies a fun, albeit no-nonsense approach in working with a wide variety of clientele, including professional and entrepreneurial women, newlyweds, couples with young children, and military families in their accumulation years. She helps all those she works with to organize and gain confidence in their financial lives.

As a financial expert, Mary Beth makes frequent appearances on NBC and has been featured in *The Wall Street Journal, Forbes, Investment News, Yahoo! Finance, MSN Money*, and more. In addition, she was named as one of the industry's 40 Under 40 for 2015 by *Investment News*.

Prior to establishing Workable Wealth, Mary Beth spent nearly 10 years in the financial services industry working with boutique and large firms alike. Most recently, she served as Director of Financial Planning with a major San Diego based Registered Investment Advisor.

You can connect with Mary Beth on Twitter and Periscope @marybstorj or on Facebook at www.Facebook.com/WorkableWealth, or through the Work Your Wealth community at www.Facebook.com/groups/WorkYourWealth.

To contact Mary Beth about media appearances or speaking at your event, or for more information, please visit www.workablewealth.com.

Made in the USA
Columbia, SC
04 January 2018